Secret Power

to Treasures, Purity,
and a Good Complexion

A Personal Bible Study on the Book of Colossians

Susie Shellenberger

ZONDERVAN™

GRAND RAPIDS, MICHIGAN 49530 USA

invert

www.invertbooks.com

Secret Power to Treasures, Purity, and a Good Complexion: A Personal Bible Study on the Book of Colossians Copyright © 2005 by Youth Specialties

Youth Specialties Products, 300 South Pierce Street, El Cajon, CA 92020, are published by Zondervan, 5300 Patterson Avenue SE, Grand Rapids, MI 49530

Library of Congress Cataloging-in-Publication Data

Shellenberger, Susie.
  Secret power to treasures, purity, and a good complexion : a personal bible study on the book of Colossians / by Susie Shellenberger.
    p. cm. -- (Secret power Bible studies)
  ISBN 0-310-25679-8 (pbk.)
  1. Bible. N.T. Colossians--Criticism, interpretation, etc. 2. Bible. N.T. Colossians--Text-books. 3. Teenage girls--Religious life. I. Title.
  BS2715.52.S54 2005
  227'.7'0071--dc22

                                                                                    2004029343

Editorial direction by Will Penner
Art direction by Holly Sharp
Edited by Maureen McNabb
Proofreading by Janie Wilkerson and Joanne Heim
Interior design by SharpSeven Design
Cover design by Burnkit
Printed in the United States of America

06 07 08 09 / DCI / 10 9 8 7 6 5 4 3 2

Table of Contents

Introduction

READ THIS FIRST!

"So what do you have?" Kylie practically shouted in the noisy school cafeteria.

Shayla dug into her sack lunch and pulled out her prize. "Leftover pepperoni pizza!" she said with a smile.

"Any chance I can talk you into trading?"

"Depends," Shayla said. "Whatcha got?"

"Bologna."

"No way!"

"But that's not all," Kylie said. "I made my famous dessert last night, and I'll even give you that too! All for just that one measly little slice of pizza."

"What famous dessert?"

"Ahhh. I haven't told anyone, because I've never made it before. But I know it's great!"

"Uh huh," Shayla said. "What is it?"

"It's my own special concoction of the best sugar cookies you'll ever eat in this lifetime."

"Oh, yeah?" Shayla's interest was rising. "You made them last night?"

"Yep."

"And how many have you eaten so far?"

"None," Kylie said. "I had to clean the kitchen after I made them, and I still had homework to do. So I didn't even have time to eat them."

"So we don't really *know* they're any good, do we?" Shayla teased. "I'm sticking with the pizza."

Kylie laughed. "Actually, you can keep the pizza and I'll still share. I brought five cookies."

"Thanks, Kylie. I'll try one in a minute. Hey, I've missed you at youth group the past couple of weeks. Do you need a ride?"

"Nah. I just haven't gone. I'm re-thinking my belief system."

"What's that mean?" Shayla asked.

"Well, we read a story about Buddhism in my humanities class," Kylie said, "and I like parts of it."

"Parts of the story, or parts of Buddhism?" Shayla pressed.

"I agree with parts of the Buddhist religion. And there's a new girl in my social studies class who's Islamic. She's been sharing her beliefs with me, and I'm discovering that I really like parts of Islam too."

"But you're a Christian, Kylie!"

"Yeah, I'm a Christian. But I think there's room to fit in a few other things that sound good too. I'm also attracted to parts of Wicca."

By now Shayla had bitten into one of Kylie's sugar cookies.

"Hey! What's with the face?" Kylie asked.

"Sorry, girlfriend," Shayla laughed. "But these cookies are to die for—literally! Like if I take another bite, I'll die!"

"No way!" Kylie grabbed a cookie and eagerly took a bite.

"Hey! What's with the face?" Shayla asked.

"Ooooh, you're right. These are *horrible*! Be glad you kept your pizza!"

"Kylie, what in the world did you put in these cookies?"

"Well, I didn't really follow a recipe."

"What?"

"Shayla, I'm tired of following someone else's instructions. I just figured I'd eaten enough sugar cookies in my life to know what would work best, and what I'd enjoy most. So I just kind of made up my own recipe."

"Didn't work, did it, Kylie?"

"This batch is definitely dead. But I'll get it right next time."

"Give it up, girl! Just follow the recipe. It's so much easier than having to guess and experiment."

"I wasn't really that far off," Kylie said. "I just threw in a few extra items and deleted some of the old routine stuff."

"Yeah? Like what?"

"Well...instead of using flour, I used baking soda—"

"What? Good grief, Kylie! Flour is the necessary ingredient in almost every cookie in the world."

"But baking soda *looks* like flour. And instead of using sugar, I used maple syrup."

"Gross."

"And instead of regular salt, I used seasoned salt."

"That explains it," Shayla said. "Your cookies turned out gross because you didn't follow the proven recipe. Kylie, you can't just take a little of this and a little of that—even though it may *look* like the ingredient you're supposed to use—and expect your cookies to turn out well."

"Okay, okay. I just wanted to experiment."

"Kinda sounds like you're wanting to experiment in your relationship with Christ too."

"Whaddya talking about?" Kylie asked.

"Listen to yourself. You're saying you want a little of Buddhism, some Wicca, and maybe even some Islam. What are you thinking?"

"I was thinking that I could add the stuff I like about those beliefs to my relationship with Christ."

"Well, you can't. Sure, Buddhism promotes goodness, but it denies that Jesus Christ is God's Son. And there are some Wiccans who say they just cast 'good spells,' but any power they have definitely doesn't come from the Holy Spirit. And yeah, Islam promotes peace, but it also promotes having to earn your salvation. The Bible says Jesus Christ is the only way to heaven—not Allah!"

"I never thought of it that way," Kylie said.

"Hey, I'm not coming down on you. I just want you to realize that when you mess with your relationship with Jesus Christ, you're messing with the most important thing in the world."

"I just didn't think there would be any harm in adding a few more things to Christianity," Kylie said.

"But that's just it," Shayla said. "When you start adding to and taking away from Christianity, it's not Christianity anymore."

"Shayla, what are you doing around 6:45 this Wednesday evening?"

"Why?"

"I'm hoping you can pick me up for youth group. I need to get back on track spiritually."

"You got it, girlfriend! And Kylie?"

"Yeah?"

"Let's go grab an ice-cream bar before class. My treat."

"Anything's better than those maple syrup, baking soda, seasoned salt death wishes," Kylie laughed.

"Ooooh. I wouldn't wish those on my worst enemy!"

Why do we sometimes insist on messing with a good thing? Maybe it's just our human nature to tinker with something to make it our own, but one thing is crystal clear: We can't mess with Christianity. The recipe is already perfect. When we subtract that Jesus Christ is the Messiah or add some rigidity and false teachings, we're doing things that lead to spiritual death.

And guess what. That's exactly what some of the Christians in the church at Colosse were doing. They, like Kylie, were confused. They were trying to add and subtract from their relationship with Christ. They had accepted false doctrine and rigid rules. They had gotten completely away from the fact that only Jesus is the true Messiah—and the only way to heaven.

Even though the apostle Paul was imprisoned in Rome, he'd heard about what was going on with the Colossians, and he wanted to help them. So he wrote this specific letter to remind them of the truths from which they had wandered.

If he was in jail, how did he find out what was going on in the church at Colosse?

Great question! His friend Epaphras, a native of Colosse, came to visit him in prison. Epaphras had founded the church in Colosse and was concerned about what was happening with many of the Christians there.

But I hear a lot of different ideas about who Jesus is.

Unless they echo what the Bible says (that Jesus is the Son of God, the true Messiah, and our only way of salvation), everything else you hear is not only false, but also dangerous!

Here's an idea: Instead of falling for all the lies about Jesus, why not discover him for *yourself!* You see, that's what the book of Colossians is all about. The apostle Paul wants to help you sift through the false messages you're bombarded with and personally introduce you to Jesus Christ.

I can get all that from the book of Colossians?

All that and more! Just as you can't combine a little of this and a little of that and leave out the essential ingredients of a proven recipe, neither can you combine false ideas and good-sounding philosophies to form your own brand of Christianity.

"Sure felt good to be back at youth group again," Kylie said.

"It sure is good to *have* you back," Shayla said. "We all missed you."

"I can't believe I got so confused about Christianity so quickly."

"You know what helps keep me on track, Kylie?"

"What?"

"The Secret Power Bible Study."

"I've heard Aimee, Pastor Jeff's wife, talk about being a Secret Power Girl. Are the two connected?"

"They sure are! Secret Power Girls are female Christians who are plugged into an incredible power source. In fact, you *could* say it's a supernatural power source."

"Wow! I want that," Kylie said. "Where do you get it?"

"It's the power of the Holy Spirit. And it's available to all Christians. I'll ask Aimee to get you the *Secret Power Girls* book, okay?"

"Yeah, I'd love that, Shayla."

"You'll want to start with that, because it explains how to be a Secret Power Girl."

"So what happens after I understand about the Holy Spirit and actually become a Secret Power Girl?" Kylie asked.

"Then you start growing and staying on the right track. And that's where the Secret Power Bible Studies come in. In fact, Aimee is leading one right now on the book of Colossians. It talks about a lot of the stuff you're going through."

"You might think this is weird, Shayla," Kylie said, "but I've never done a Bible study before. What is it?"

"I don't think that's weird at all. I hadn't done one either, until Aimee helped me get plugged into the Secret Power Bible Studies. They're really fun. Everything's all broken up into bite-size chunks that you can easily do every single day by yourself. After you've completed an entire chapter of the Bible, you meet with our group for accountability."

"Okay. Now I'm totally lost. What's accountability?"

Shayla smiled. "It sounds confusing, doesn't it? But it's really not. Accountability means that you allow another person or small group of people to pray with you and for you, and to ask you questions about the tough stuff in your life to help you stay on the right track spiritually."

"Wow! I totally need that!"

"We have a small group of girls—five of us—who meet weekly with Aimee. We've already done one Secret Power Bible Study. We just completed the book of Philippians. Right now we're beginning Colossians. So I'll get you the *Secret Power Girl* book (you really ought to read that first), and you can start the Colossians Bible study with us this week!"

"Thanks, Shayla! But what about that study on Philippians that I already missed?"

"Go ahead and get the book. When we finish our Secret Power Bible Study on Colossians, I'll do Philippians with you."

"But you've already done it."

"Yeah, but it's really fun. And I'd love for just the two of us to do it together."

"Count me in, Shayla!"

You can either do this study alone, or you can grab a friend to do it with you. *Or*, like Kylie and Shayla, you can ask an adult female to lead a small group of four or five girls that will meet weekly to complete the study.

At the end of each chapter, you'll be challenged to grab a friend (accountability), memorize some Scripture, and record your thoughts, prayer requests, and answers to prayer in a journal section.

Don't Wait!

So back to the conflicting ideas about Jesus...why accept substitutes when you can have the real thing? Jesus Christ is definitely the real thing! He always has been and always will be!

So pull on your hiking boots. We're about to take an exciting journey through the book of Colossians.

Your Secret Power Sister,

Susie Shellenberger

Christ: The Energizer!

(Note: Each chapter of this Bible study is divided into bite-size chunks that you can either swallow all at once or spread out and complete over a period of time. Try to complete one entire bite at each sitting, okay?)

Colossians

Where is it? In the New Testament, immediately after Philippians and just before 1 Thessalonians.

Who wrote it? Paul.

Who was he? Paul was an apostle of Jesus Christ, but he sure took an interesting route in getting there! He used to hate Christians. In fact, he even persecuted them. But God temporarily blinded him and helped him see that what he was doing was wrong. When that happened, Paul gave his life to God. You can read the whole story in Acts 9. After Paul began serving God, he wrote several letters (books of the New Testament) to fellow Christians. This book of Colossians is a letter he wrote to the church in the city of Colosse.

BITE #1

Paul, an apostle of Christ Jesus by the will of God, and Timothy our brother, to the holy and faithful brothers in Christ at Colosse: Grace and peace to you from God our Father. (Colossians 1:1-2)

What's an apostle?

_____ A. A figurine for a new game by Milton Bradley.

_____ B. One of the original 12 disciples, plus Matthias and Paul.

_____ C. A Bible professor at Bethlehem Community College.

_____ D. One who pours concrete for swimming pools.

The apostles were the original 12 disciples chosen by Jesus. After Judas Iscariot betrayed Christ and died, the disciples met together and prayed for someone to take his place. *Matthias* was chosen. Later, after Saul dedicated his life to Christ and his name was changed to *Paul*, he also joined the rank of apostles.

But everyone who follows Jesus Christ is considered a disciple. How does that make you feel? (Check all that apply.)

_____ A. Pretty special   _____ C. Honored

_____ B. Frightened   _____ D. Reluctant

We always thank God, the Father of our Lord Jesus Christ, when we pray for you, because we have heard of your faith in Christ Jesus and of the love you have for all the saints—the faith and love that spring from the hope that is stored up for you in heaven and that you have already heard about in the word of truth, the gospel that has come to you. (Colossians 1:3-5)

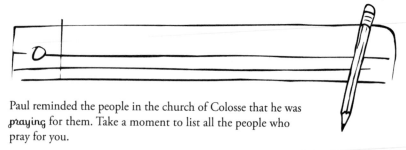

Paul reminded the people in the church of Colosse that he was *praying* for them. Take a moment to list all the people who pray for you.

Are you aware that Jesus Christ prays for you? In fact, before he was crucified, he prayed an *incredibly special prayer* for you. Grab your own Bible and flip to John 17. What are some specific things Jesus talks to God about on your behalf?

Are there people for whom you pray *regularly*? If so, list their names in the space provided. If not, write a prayer asking God to bring specific people to your mind for whom God wants you to pray.

Paul also mentions the "hope that is stored up for you in heaven." Sometimes we need to be reminded that heaven is our *real* home. Heaven is where we'll live eternally. We'll never get sick in heaven; *we won't suffer;* and we'll never experience any problems. Wow! Think about it: You'll never be *lonely,* jealous, picked on, made fun of, or have to worry about how you look (because you'll get a brand-new spiritual body)! We'll also get to live forever with God, who created us. *That* is our hope.

If you truly looked at life through this perspective, how would that change the daily problems you face? (Check all that apply.)

_____ A. It would make my trials seem smaller.
_____ B. It would give me more confidence, because I'd realize I have
            something much greater to look forward to.
_____ C. It would give me true joy.
_____ D. I'd probably worry less about how I look.
_____ E. Other _____

BITE #2

All over the world this gospel is producing fruit and growing, just as it has been doing among you since the day you heard it and understood God's grace in all its truth. (Colossians 1:6)

Paul *wasn't afraid* to preach the gospel. In fact, he shared the Good News everywhere he went. He talked about God when he was in *jail,* while he was being *persecuted,* and on a shipwrecked *island.* Because his relationship with Jesus *consumed* him, it was always the topic of his conversation with others.

What about you? Is your relationship with Christ *so important* to you that you can't help but talk about it? Take this quick quiz and rate your *talkability* regarding God.

Is Christ Showing?

1. My friends know I'm a Christian, because I talk about Christ in many of our conversations.

    _____ True   _____ False

2. Most of my classmates know I'm a Christian, because of my conversation and my actions.

    _____ True   _____ False

3. I discuss what God is teaching me with my family.

    _____ True   _____ False

4. I share prayer requests with my friends.

    _____ True   _____ False

5. I talk about church and youth group activities with those around me.

    _____ True   _____ False

6. Even people who don't know me personally would suspect I'm a Christian because of the way I act.

    _____ True   _____ False

7. If a stranger eavesdropped on most of my conversations, she would guess I'm a Christian because of what I talk about.

    _____ True   _____ False

8. I can't wait to share answers to prayer with my friends or family members.

    _____ True   _____ False

9. I'm not ashamed to carry my Bible to school.

    _____ True   _____ False

10. One of my favorite things to talk about with others is my relationship with God.

    _____ True   _____ False

How did you do? Is Christ showing through your life? Is it obvious to others that you're in love with Jesus? If you need help in this area, take a moment to write out a prayer in the space provided asking God to help you reflect your relationship with God more to those around you.

If you're a shining reflection of Christ's love right now, write him a prayer asking for specific opportunities to share him with those who aren't Christians.

You learned it from Epaphras, our dear fellow servant, who is a faithful minister of Christ on our behalf, and who also told us of your love in the Spirit. (Colossians 1:7-8)

Many *Bible scholars* think Epaphras founded the church in Colosse while Paul was living in Ephesus (see Acts 19:10). Epaphras visited Paul in *prison* and told him about the problems happening in the Colossian church. Their conversation is what motivated Paul to write this letter to the Colossians.

Read Colossians 1:7-8 again. What kind of reputation did Epaphras have?

What kind of reputation do *you* have? (Circle all that apply.)

As a Christian, you—like Epaphras—are considered a minister of Christ. In other words, God wants you to *share* the Good News with those around you, take your relationship with Jesus seriously, and be *faithful* to him. What would it take to for others to view you as a "faithful minister of Christ," as Paul saw Epaphras?

———— A. I'd need to establish an actual relationship with Christ.

———— B. I'd need to get more serious about my relationship with Christ.

———— C. I'd need to be more vocal about my relationship with Christ.

———— D. I'd need to deepen my relationship with Christ.

———— E. Other ————————————

BITE #3

For this reason, since the day we heard about you, we have not stopped praying for you and asking God to fill you with the knowledge of his will through all spiritual wisdom and understanding. (Colossians 1:9)

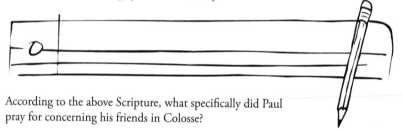

According to the above Scripture, what specifically did Paul pray for concerning his friends in Colosse?

What specifically do you most often pray for when you pray for your friends?

What specifically do you most often pray for when you pray for your family members?

Read Colossians 1:9 again. According to this verse...

_____ A. We can know a fraction of God's will for our lives.

_____ B. We can have a little portion of God's wisdom.

_____ C. If we work really hard at being good and give more money
to our church, we can know what God wants us to do.

_____ D. We can actually know God's will for our lives.

Let's chat about wisdom for a few minutes. Grab your own Bible and flip to Proverbs 10:14. Read the Scripture and jot down what a wise person will do.

Now flip back to Proverbs 4:5. What things does this Scripture encourage you to "get" or learn to develop?

And according to Proverbs 4:6, what are the benefits of clinging to wisdom?

Check out what Proverbs 4:11 says in _The Living Bible_: "A life of doing right is the wisest life there is."

If the Great Physician (Jesus) were to give you a spiritual examination right now, how would your "check-up" go, according to this verse?

BITE #4

And we pray this in order that you may live a life worthy of the Lord and may please him in every way: bearing fruit in every good work, growing in the knowledge of God, being strengthened with all power according to his glorious might so that you may have great endurance and patience, and joyfully giving thanks to the Father, who has qualified you to share in the inheritance of the saints in the kingdom of light. (Colossians 1:10-12)

Paul had never met the Colossians, but oh, how he prayed for them! And according to the above verses, he prayed a mighty prayer! You, too, can pray for people you've never met. Make a list of people you don't know personally but for whom you should pray. I'll get you started; you complete the list.

1. The president of our country

2.

3. Missionaries

4.

5.

6.

7.

8. Those in need you hear about on the news or read about in the paper

According to what Paul prayed for the Colossians, how can you obtain great endurance and patience?

In what areas of your life do you need endurance and patience?

teachers money
my relationship with Mom & Dad my friends PEER PRESSURE
locker partner schoolwork GRADES
my dog NEIGHBORS
my personal struggles what I start youth group
THOSE WHO TALK ABOUT ME finishing other: discipline studying
habits

Paul prayed that the Colossians would "grow in the knowledge of God." What will it take for *you* to *grow spiritually* in this manner? (Check all that apply.)

_____ A. I'll need to read my Bible more.

_____ B. I'll need to go shopping.

_____ C. I'll start praying more often.

_____ D. I'll get more involved in church and youth group.

_____ E. I'll watch more TV.

_____ F. I'll talk about my faith with others.

_____ G. I'll memorize our church bulletin.

_____ H. Other _____

"...and joyfully giving thanks to the Father, who has qualified you to share in the inheritance of the saints in the kingdom of light." (Colossians 1:12)

How long has it been since you've thanked God for the blessings you've received? Have you ever thanked God for what Paul suggests—the fact that you get "to share in the inheritance of the saints in the kingdom of light"?

Take a few minutes to design some creative bumper sticker slogans expressing your thankfulness to God for a variety of things.

THANKS, GOD! I OWE YOU MY LIFE!

BITE #5

For he has rescued us from the dominion of darkness and brought us into the kingdom of the Son he loves, in whom we have redemption, the forgiveness of sins. (Colossians 1:13-14)

Flash back to your younger years. Identify things from the list below that frightened you as a child.

In addition to some of the above, many children are also afraid of *darkness*. The people in the Colossian church were afraid of the *unseen forces of darkness*. What *are* the unseen forces of darkness?

_____ A. Whatever's living under your bed.

_____ B. The stuff inside the bathtub drain.

_____ C. Satan and his demonic forces.

_____ D. Anything that makes a weird noise.

You can't see Satan and his demons, but we know they're at work, because the Bible is clear on the fact that *Satan hates you*, and his mission is to destroy you.

Check this out: "For we are not fighting against people made of flesh and blood, but against persons without bodies—the evil rulers of the unseen world, those mighty satanic beings and great evil princes of darkness who rule this world; and against huge numbers of wicked spirits in the spirit world" (Ephesians 6:12, *The Living Bible*).

As Christians, we should be *aware* of Satan's tactics so we can guard against them. But we need to be careful not to become obsessed or fearful of them. Satan can play on our *curiosity*. Those who say, "I just want to find out what Satanism is all about" are soon in over their heads. God doesn't want us to be curious about the forces of darkness; he wants our curiosity directed *toward Jesus*. God wants to fill our curious appetites with Christ's truth—not the enemy.

Paul is reminding the Colossians that *before* they made a decision to follow Christ, they were living in *darkness*. But now that Christ ruled their lives, they *no longer* had to live in fear. Neither do you!

1 John 4:4 is a terrific verse to memorize and quote to yourself when you are fearful. Take a second to read it right now and copy it in the space provided.

Through Christ's death on the cross—and through his forgiveness of your sins—he has offered you a place in his Kingdom. He's made you a part of *his family*. You're no longer part of Satan's world of darkness; you're a child of *light*. Since you now *belong to him*, you don't need to live in fear of Satan.

He is the image of the invisible God, the firstborn over all creation. (Colossians 1:15)

Why does Paul say that Christ was the "firstborn"? We know that Jesus wasn't actually the first human being ever born. Paul was a Jew, and in Jewish culture the "firstborn" didn't necessarily mean the order of physical birth. The "firstborn" was a term used by Jews to mean great honor. By referring to Christ as the "firstborn," Paul was reminding the Colossians that Jesus is honored over all creation.

Grab your Bible and check out Psalm 89:27.

What is David called in this verse?

Now flip to Exodus 4:22. How is Israel referred to in this Scripture?

Have you ever wondered what God looks like? According to the above verse, you can know the description of God by looking at the life of Jesus. Pretend you've been contacted by *The New York Times* to write a character description of God. All you have to rely on are paintings you've seen of Jesus, the Bible, and your personal relationship with Christ. Go ahead. Based on all you know about Jesus, take *The New York Times* up on its offer and jot down your description below.

We can actually know God by...

———— A. Taking a photo of the sky.

———— B. Knowing Jesus.

———— C. Walking past several churches.

———— D. Chanting, "I know God, I know God, I know God" and later setting it to music.

BITE #6

For by him all things were created: things in heaven and on earth, visible and invisible, whether thrones or powers or rulers or authorities; all things were created by him and for him. (Colossians 1:16)

What does the above verse tell you about God's power?

The Colossian Christians were confused. They doubted that God actually created the entire world, because the world contains evil. How could a perfect God create evil?

Everything God created was good, but God also chooses to allow us free will. In other words, God lets us choose to do right or to do wrong. Unfortunately, we don't always make the right choice. Some of us have chosen to do evil things; some have even chosen to become evil people.

In fact, some of the angels in heaven didn't make the right choice, either. Satan (Lucifer) was an angel whom God blessed with many musical gifts. But because God doesn't treat angels (or people) like puppets, forcing them to move, act, and decide the way God wants them to, Lucifer made the bad choice of disobeying God. He became jealous and wanted God's power. He desired equal status with the Creator.

But there can only be one King of Kings. There is only one God. One Creator. No one is God's equal. And since God's Kingdom is perfect, God can't allow sin in heaven. So God threw Satan out of heaven. Several angels (also making bad choices and known as demons) followed Satan, and they've been wreaking havoc on earth ever since.

But although sin is in the world, *God's power* isn't weaker. God hasn't become lessened because of evil. God is still in control. God is still on the throne and *always* will be. The Bible assures us that someday, God will allow Jesus to permanently defeat Satan and his demons for *eternity*.

What if someone approached you and said, "If God is a good God and full of love, why is there evil in the world?" How would you respond?

BITE #7

How do you feel when friends ask you religious questions you're not sure how to answer?

_____ A. It makes me determined to study, do the research necessary and find the answers.

_____ B. I get really, really frustrated really, really fast.

_____ C. I usually spend some time in prayer and seek God's direction on how to respond.

_____ D. I make up something if I don't know the answer.

Here are a couple of great books to read that will help you understand and defend your faith: *The Case for Faith* and *The Case for Christ*, both by Lee Strobel. Both have student editions published by Zondervan and can be ordered through any Christian bookstore.

It's easy to get *frustrated* when our friends don't agree with our religious beliefs. Paul patiently *listened* to the Colossians' arguments, and then he gave them *correct information*. Often, it's not a matter of friends wanting to pick a fight, but rather friends being *confused* and really wanting the truth.

As we mentioned in the introduction to this book, Paul wrote this particular letter to the Christians in Colosse to address a *specific problem*. There were people in the Colossian church who were confused and followed a different set of beliefs from what Paul preached. These people were known as *Gnostics*—which means "the intellectual ones."

They didn't want to accept the simplicity of Christianity. They wanted to turn Christianity into a *philosophy* they could blend with other religious philosophies. But Christianity isn't a philosophy; *it's a way of life.* It's all about having a personal, growing *relationship* with Jesus Christ. So Paul *confidently* restated some of the *basics* of Christianity and our core beliefs—as seen in Colossians 1:16-20.

What are some other mistaken views people have of Christianity today?

The gospel is actually...

_____ A. Simple.   _____ C. A fairy tale.

_____ B. Extremely hard to grasp.   _____ D. A love story.

Guess what? The gospel is a very *simple love story.* Though many try to intellectualize it and make it more difficult than it is, it's really the *beautiful truth* of God loving us so much that he willingly sent his only son to pay the *death penalty* for our sins. How does that make you feel?

Are you glad you don't have to be a genius to understand the gospel? Take a moment to write God a letter thanking him for the simplicity of the gospel.

BITE #8

He is before all things, and in him all things hold together. (Colossians 1:17)

Grab your Bible and check out Revelation 1:8. What do that verse and Colossians 1:17 have in common?

Before you put your Bible down, flip to John 1:1. What is associated with being with God in the beginning?

It's hard for our human minds to imagine how God could always *be*. We naturally want to assign a beginning and an end to all things. But the Bible clearly tells us that God and God's Word always were. And to help us grasp this truth, we're told that the *beginning* of beginning lies inside God. God created beginnings, and God is in charge of the finale.

Knowing that God is in charge of the start and finish of my life...

_____ A. Makes me more comfortable.

_____ B. Scares me to death.

_____ C. Makes me want to do everything to God's glory.

_____ D. Gives me confidence.

_____ E. Causes me to get more serious about my relationship with God.

Paul also reminds the Colossians that Christ holds all things together. List the top three things you desperately need God to hold together right now in your life.

1.

2.

3.

We tend to think of spiritual things when we think of God. And while it's true that God holds all spiritual things together—and that God has reconciled humans with himself through Jesus—God also holds the physical universe together. Think about it: God is the one who decides how far the waves roll and how high the tide grows. God decides how often the rain will fall, when it will snow, and how many galaxies exist.

Scientists have done a great job explaining much of the mystery of our world, but only God can explain the why. Only God understands how the universe was created.

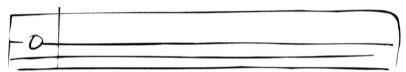

Grab your Bible again and flip back to the Old Testament. Read Job 38:4-12. What questions of the physical universe are asked?

Now check out verses 13-27. What questions are asked in these verses?

Take a peek at Job 38:28-41.

∗   What does God ask about the lightning?

∗   What does he ask about lions?

∗   What's mentioned about the seasons and the stars?

Grab your Bible and read Job chapter 39. What does this tell you about God's creativity?

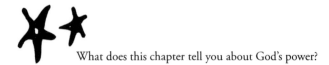

What does this chapter tell you about God's power?

Let's read Colossians 1:17 again:

He is before all things, and in him all things hold together.

After reading the above Scripture, and after reading portions of the book of Job, what parallels can you draw?

BITE #9

And he is the head of the body, the church; he is the beginning and the firstborn from among the dead, so that in everything he might have the supremacy. (Colossians 1:18)

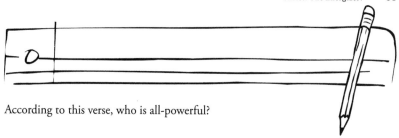

According to this verse, who is all-powerful?

List people in today's society to whom we tend to assign power or greatness.

When we know that God ultimately holds all power, why do we often fail to acknowledge his power, and instead turn to others in our society?

Paul mentions that Christ is the "firstborn from among the dead." It's because of Christ's resurrection that Christianity is set apart from all other religious beliefs. Think about it: If Christ hadn't risen from the dead, Christianity would hold no more power than Hinduism, Buddhism, or Islam. And because Christ actually conquered death...

_____ A. Christians, too, will someday conquer death by living eternally with him.

_____ B. We can boldly say "nyah, nyah, nyah, nyah, nyah" to anyone professing a different religious belief from ours.

_____ C. We no longer have to do homework.

_____ D. We don't have to pay for car insurance.

For God was pleased to have all his fullness dwell in him, and through him to reconcile to himself all things, whether things on earth or things in heaven, by making peace through his blood, shed on the cross. (Colossians 1:19-20)

What does it mean "to reconcile"?

_____ A. It's a thing relatives do.

_____ B. It means to bridge the distance.

_____ C. It's cooking with Italian ingredients and serving something over chocolate.

_____ D. To get sick.

Check out the following scenario and jot down your ideas on how Anna can reconcile her differences with Whitney.

"I just don't understand her!" Anna said to her mom. "Whitney knows I've had a crush on Bryan for like...forever. And today I found out that he asked her to the all-school carnival on Friday. She's supposed to be my best friend! I've told her all my secrets. How could she do this to me?"

"Did she accept Bryan's invitation to go to the carnival?" Mom asked.

"Yes. Well...probably. I mean, I don't know for sure. But why wouldn't she? He's the coolest guy in school. Who wouldn't want to go with him?"

"Is it really her fault that Bryan asked her to the carnival?"

"She was probably flirting with him. She's always smiling at people!"

"Smiling at someone and flirting are two different things, Anna."

"Well, I don't care. It ticks me off! She's supposed to be my best friend."

"And she still is."

"Not if she's going to the carnival with the guy I'm crushing on!"

"Anna, you don't know enough about the situation to be making these kinds of judgments. Why don't you give Whitney a call and work out your differences?"

Anna was so mad she could hardly think.

What can she do to reconcile things with her friend?

Because God has reconciled differences with you through Christ, God wants you to reconcile your differences with others. List anyone you can think of with whom you need to build a bridge.

Once you were alienated from God and were enemies in your minds because of your evil behavior. (Colossians 1:21)

List as many adjectives as you can think of to identify how you'd feel if you could never be reconciled with God because of your sin. (I'll toss in a few to get you started; you complete the space provided.)

Isolated

Hopeless

Alone

But now he has reconciled you by Christ's physical body through death to present you holy in his sight, without blemish and free from accusation—if you continue in your faith, established and firm, not moved from the hope held out in the gospel. This is the gospel that you heard and that has been proclaimed to every creature under heaven, and of which I, Paul, have become a servant. (Colossians 1:22-23)

When someone is pronounced "not guilty" in a court of law, it's as though that person has never even been accused. The only way to stand "not guilty" in God's sight is by asking for and accepting Christ's forgiveness for your sins. Have you asked Christ to forgive your sins?

_____ Yes   _____ No   _____ I can't remember

If you've never repented of your sins and asked Christ to forgive you, God still considers you "guilty." But there's good news! Grab your Bible, and check out Romans 3:22. According to this verse, what can you gain through faith in Christ?

If you've never repented of your sins and sought Christ's forgiveness, you can do so right now by praying this prayer:

> *God, I realize I was born a sinner. I've done things I shouldn't have done, and I've broken your heart. I've run my own life when I should have yielded to your control. Please forgive me for my sins. I realize you love me so much that you actually died for my sins. Jesus, I don't deserve that kind of love! I should have been the one who paid the penalty for sinning. But you chose to take my place. Thank you, Jesus! Thank you!*
>
> *I give my life to you. I want you to reign and rule and guide every aspect of my life. I want to please you. I want to bring glory to you. I want to live eternally in heaven with you.*
>
> *Thank you for your precious forgiveness of my sins. Thank you for declaring me "not guilty" when I will someday stand in your presence. Thank you for wiping my slate clean—as if I'd never sinned.*
>
> *I love you, Jesus.*
>
> *In your name I pray, Amen.*

BITE #10

Now I rejoice in what was suffered for you, and I fill up in my flesh what is still lacking in regard to Christ's afflictions, for the sake of his body, which is the church. (Colossians 1:24)

Paul tells the Colossians that he rejoices in the fact that Christ suffered and died for them. You, too, can rejoice and celebrate the fact that Christ suffered and died for your family and friends. We're grateful for Christ's death, but we also celebrate his resurrection from the dead! He's alive right now! He didn't simply die for your sins; he rose and lives to empower you to live the holy life he calls you to live!

Paul also tells his friends in Colosse that he, too, will suffer in spreading the gospel. Christ never promised us that being a Christian would be easy. When we take the gospel to the world around us, we're unable to avoid suffering.

What are some of the things you find toughest about sharing your faith with others?

Which types of suffering have you experienced because of your determination to share the gospel with others? (Check all that apply.)

_____ A. People have made fun of me.

_____ B. I've been physically abused.

_____ C. I've been jailed.

_____ D. People have told lies about me.

_____ E. I've been falsely accused.

_____ F. I've been sent to the principal's office.

_____ G. I've been given detention.

_____ H. I've been verbally abused.

_____ I. I've been laughed at.

_____ J. People have talked about me behind my back.

_____ K. Some people refuse to be my friends.

Take a moment to stop and *pray for missionaries*—those who have committed their lives to spreading the gospel in other countries. Many of them face daily persecution. Ask God to *empower* them and guide their steps.

Now take a moment to *write out a prayer* for Christians living in countries who oppose Christianity. Many of these Christians are *taken* from their families, beaten, jailed, or even killed. Ask God to strengthen and comfort them. Pray for the *persecution to cease.*

I have become its servant by the commission God gave me to present

to you the word of God in its fullness—the mystery that has been kept hidden for ages and generations, but is now disclosed to the saints. (Colossians 1:25-26)

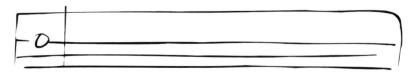

What does it mean to be "commissioned"?

As a Christian, you are commissioned by God to share your faith with others. What are some specific ways you can do this?

To them God has chosen to make known among the Gentiles the glorious riches of this mystery, which is Christ in you, the hope of glory. (Colossians 1:27)

When we stop and think about it, it's mind-boggling to realize the very Maker of Creation, the One who holds the stars in the sky and placed order in the universe, actually lives inside of us!

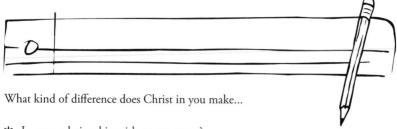

What kind of difference does Christ in you make...

✴ In your relationship with your parents?

* In your relationship with your siblings?

* In your friendships?

* In your dating relationships?

* In your actions?

* In your reactions?

* In your habits?

* In your trials?

* In your goals?

We proclaim him, admonishing and teaching everyone with all wisdom, so that we may present everyone perfect in Christ. (Colossians 1:28)

The confused Christians in the Colossian church proclaimed that no human could be perfect. But if we allow a perfect Christ to saturate our lives, he can perfect our hearts! That doesn't mean we'll always act perfectly, but our desire to serve Christ and become all he wants us to be can be perfect. And when we live eternally with him, we'll join him in perfection. We'll have a perfect body, a perfect attitude, and a perfect spirit.

What response would Christ have you give to someone who says, "You think you're perfect just because you're a Christian!"

To this end I labor, struggling with all his energy, which so powerfully works in me. (Colossians 1:29)

Using as many adjectives as you can think of, list descriptive words of God. I'll toss out a few to get you started; you fill in the space provided.

Powerful   Perfect

                    All-Knowing   Compassionate
Loving

               Forgiving   Wise

     Healer   Counselor

Have you ever thought of God as being energetic? God is all-powerful—full of more energy than we can even imagine! Knowing that Christ's mighty energy is at work within you, how should that affect your attitude when you're tired of doing what's right?

Whatever you do—whether it's running track, singing, encouraging others, or making good grades—you can only do it as long as Christ continues to give you strength. Paul recognized Christ as his strength source. Have you realized that your strength, your gifts, and your abilities all come from Christ?

Let's look at this same Scripture from a few other versions of the Bible:

"This is my work, and I can do it only because Christ's mighty energy is at work within me." *(The Living Bible)*

"To get this done I toil and struggle, using the mighty strength which Christ supplies and which is at work in me." *(Today's English Version)*

"That's why I'm working so hard day after day, year after year, doing my best with the energy God so graciously gives me." *(The Message)*

"To this end I also labor, striving according to his working which works in me mightily." *(New King James)*

Paraphrase (rewrite in your own words) Colossians 1:29.

BITE #11

GRAB A FRIEND

Congratulations! You just completed the first chapter of Colossians. How does it feel to be a Secret Power Girl who is learning how to apply God's Word to her life? Now grab a friend and discuss the following questions together:

* Are there areas in my faith in which I'm confused or which contradict simple Christianity?

* What kind of reputation do I have with people in my church? In my neighborhood? At my school? In my community?

* What have I done this past week to reflect Christ?

* With whom have I made an effort to reconcile—work things out with, build a bridge—this week? (Or is there someone with whom I've been avoiding this?)

* How am I living out my commission from Christ?

MEMORIZE IT!

Try to memorize this verse with your friend and say it to each other the next time you get together:

For he has rescued us from the dominion of darkness and brought us into the kingdom of the Son he loves, in whom we have redemption, the forgiveness of sins. (Colossians 1:13-14)

MY JOURNAL

Okay, S.P.G. This is your space, so take advantage of it. You can do whatever you want with this space, but always try to include the following:

* List your prayer requests. (Later, as God answers them, go back and write in the date God answered your prayer.)

* Copy down any verse we studied in the previous chapter that you don't understand, and let this be a reminder to ask your parents, your Sunday School teacher, pastor, or youth leader about it.

* Jot down what stood out the most from this chapter.

Treasure Hunt!

BITE #1

I want you to know how much I am struggling for you and for those at Laodicea, and for all who have not met me personally. (Colossians 2:1)

What a special glimpse we get into Paul's tender heart as he begins the second chapter of this letter to the people in Colosse. He's never met the Colossians or the Laodiceans, yet he's aware of their confusion. And he *hurts* for them. He tells them he's struggling for them.

Remember, when Paul wrote this letter he was in *prison*! But instead of being self-centered and thinking about his own hardship, he focused instead on the needs of *others*.

Laodicea was a city just a few miles from Colosse. Bible scholars believe the Laodicean church—like the church in Colosse—had been started by one of Paul's converts. Laodicea was a wealthy city and a hub of trade and commerce. But simply because there was a growing church in Laodicea didn't mean the Christians in the church were spiritually strong.

Let's take a peek at what the *apostle John* later wrote about the Laodicean Christians. *Grab your Bible* and turn to the very last book—Revelation 3:14-22.

The apostle John is criticizing the believers in Laodicea for being...

_____ A. Short.	_____ C. Snotty.
_____ B. Tall.	_____ D. Lukewarm.

Maybe you're familiar with the old tale "The Frog and the Kettle." It states that you can place a frog in a kettle of boiling water, and he'll immediately jump out. If frogs could think, he'd be thinking, *Owwww! That's really, really, really hot! Gotta get out.*

But you can place a frog in a kettle of lukewarm water—water that's room temperature—and he'll be very comfortable. Ever so slowly, though, you could increase the intensity of the heat until finally the water in the kettle is boiling. The frog will remain in the kettle and eventually die, never understanding why. He becomes accustomed to the increasing heat and doesn't realize what's happening to him.

The apostle John saw the Laodicean Christians in the same light. They had become spiritually comfortable. They weren't on fire for Christ. They weren't intense in their faith. Yet they weren't completely cold, either. They still *had* faith, and they still professed a relationship with God. But they were simply standing still. They weren't growing spiritually. John referred to this state as being lukewarm.

That's a dangerous place to be spiritually. Jesus calls us to be totally sold-out to him. He wants to move us away from being wishy-washy casual Christians; he wants to empower us to become holy disciples.

So let's pause for a second and take your spiritual temperature. Are you hot, lukewarm, or cold? The first option in each scenario will be a hot response. The second option will be a lukewarm response. And the third option will be a cold response. Check the response that best describes your spiritual condition:

1. _____ A. God is the first thing on my mind when I wake up, and the last thing on my mind when I go to bed. (HOT)

   _____ B. I usually think about God a few times during the day. (LUKEWARM)

   _____ C. I think about God a couple of times each week or less. (COLD)

2. _____ A. I read my Bible consistently.

   _____ B. I read my Bible once a week.

   _____ C. I read my Bible a few times throughout the year.

3. _____ A. I'm plugged into a church/youth group/Bible study and attend regularly.

   _____ B. I go to church kinda sorta semi-regularly.

   _____ C. I get to church around Christmas and Easter.

4. _____ A. I'm growing spiritually, and I'm excited about what God is teaching me.

_____ B. I'm not really growing at all. I'm spiritually standing still.

_____ C. I'm taking some spiritual backward steps.

5. _____ A. If I were to die tonight, I know I'd spend eternity with God.

_____ B. I'm not sure if I'm headed toward heaven.

_____ C. I don't think I'll ever know for sure where I'll spend eternity.

6. _____ A. I love Jesus. He's my life!

_____ B. Well, I consider myself a Christian.

_____ C. I prayed a few times, but I know I'm not currently living the way God wants me to.

7. _____ A. I try to reflect Christ in everything I do.

_____ B. Every now and then I do something nice for someone.

_____ C. I'm pretty self-centered.

8. _____ A. I share my faith with others.

_____ B. If someone asked me about my faith, I'd probably admit to having faith, but I'm not going to volunteer any information.

_____ C. I never talk about my faith. If someone asked me, I'd be embarrassed to admit anything spiritual.

9. _____ A. I pray about my media choices and strive to make decisions that God would be pleased with.

_____ B. I see any movie I want to and choose my own music library. But sometimes I feel a little guilty about some of my decisions.

_____ C. What I watch and listen to is nobody's business but mine.

10. _____ A. I like to be in style, but I'm careful not to wear something that would cause a guy to be tempted.

_____ B. If a guy is tempted by what I'm wearing, it's his fault—not mine.

_____ C. I try to dress in ways that will bring attention to myself and cause guys to notice me. I don't think this has anything to do with my relationship with Christ.

So how'd you do? Were you mostly hot, lukewarm, or cold? Though there's really not a written test you can take to accurately gauge your spiritual temperature, hopefully these questions made you think more *seriously* about your relationship with Christ. If you want to know specifically where you stand with him, pray this prayer:

> *God, is there anything in my life that's not pleasing to you? If so, please bring it to my mind right now. Make me very aware of it, so I can seek your forgiveness and commit this area to you. I don't want to be a lukewarm Christian. Neither do I want to become spiritually cold. I want to be intensely focused on you. I want to be an on-fire disciple—spiritually hot! In your name I pray, Amen.*

Paul hurt for the Laodicean Christians. Remember, he wrote this letter to the Colossians because *false teaching* had occurred in their church. The Christians in Colosse were confused and were incorporating *incorrect philosophies* into Christianity. Paul wrote this letter—this book of the Bible—to clarify things and to lovingly *straighten out* the confused Christians.

Because he wanted this letter to be shared with the Laodicean Christians, he hints that false teaching had spread to their church as well. Paul is so concerned about the Christians who have become confused and weak in their faith that he tells them he's *struggling* for them even though they've never met.

Have you ever been so spiritually burdened for someone that you "struggled" for him or her?

———   Yes

———   No (If so, describe your struggle in the space provided. If no, write a prayer asking God to give you a burden for someone who's spiritually confused or who doesn't know Christ.)

What a *struggle* this must have been for Paul! He longed to personally visit Colosse and face the *false teachers* himself. It's easy to imagine how he would have loved bringing the confused Christians together to *clarify* things for them. But he was in *jail*.

So Paul *struggled through prayer* for the Christians in Colosse. He was imprisoned; he couldn't get to them. So he left the situation in God's hands.

When you're separated from someone you care about, and you know that person is going through a tough time, how do you respond?

_____ A. I worry a lot.

_____ B. I write letters, send e-mails, and make phone calls.

_____ C. I pray and ask God to intervene.

_____ D. I make myself busy and try not to think about it.

BITE #2

My purpose is that they may be encouraged in heart and united in love, so that they may have the full riches of complete understanding, in order that they may know the mystery of God, namely, Christ, in whom are hidden all the treasures of wisdom and knowledge. (Colossians 2:2-3)

Remember, Paul was writing to Christians who were being influenced by false teachers. Paul hoped that the bonds of love would bring these Christians together and cause them to stand in unity against the false teaching they were receiving.

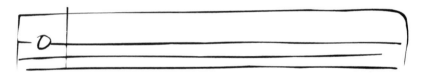

Unity often symbolizes strength. Maybe you've heard "united we stand, divided we fall." What does this mean?

Paul also prayed that the believers would be encouraged. In other words, his desire was that they be filled with courage and given renewed hope. List specific ways you can encourage (give courage and renew hope) someone who needs it.

Paul also said he wants the Christians to be united in love. Love and unity are signs of a healthy church. Think about your youth group. If teens are striving for unity, there aren't many cliques. If teens are genuinely loving one another, there's a demonstration of reaching out, welcoming newcomers, and being nice. This is a healthy group.

But when a group is full of cliques, and newcomers don't feel welcome, and gossip abounds, the group is unhealthy. What, specifically, can *you* do to help your youth group become healthier?

Let's read the verse again:

My purpose is that they may be encouraged in heart and united in love, so that they may have the full riches of complete understanding, in order that they may know the mystery of God, namely, Christ, in whom are hidden all the treasures of wisdom and knowledge. (Colossians 2:2-3)

Paul wants us to have complete understanding of our faith. Of course, this is a process. Flash back to the first grade. Your teacher didn't stand in front of the class and say, "We're going to start learning numbers now, and by the end of your first-grade year, you'll have a complete understanding of math."

You probably began learning addition and subtraction in first grade and may not have tackled multiplication and division until third or fourth grade. And you were probably a little older when you headed toward fractions. A few years down the road, you discovered equations and algebra. (Some of you may have even discovered geometry and trig.)

Okay, back to first grade. By the end of the year, you were beginning to understand math, but you didn't have a full understanding of the subject. For most of us, it's still a work in progress! Try to parallel Christianity to this example.

As a young Christian, you're beginning to understand the Bible, your faith, and the power available to you in Christ. But you don't yet have a complete understanding. Your relationship with Jesus is a work in progress. You'll continue to grow spiritually the rest of your life!

Let's take a peek at 1 Corinthians 13:12:

Now we see but a poor reflection as in a mirror; then we shall see face to face. Now I know in part; then I shall know fully, even as I am fully known.

Paul also wrote 1 and 2 Corinthians, so he's the author of the above Scripture. Jot down your thoughts on how this verse reflects what we're talking about from Colossians 2:2-3—about your complete understanding being a work in progress. When we live eternally with Christ in heaven, we'll...

_____ A. Get to jump on a trampoline forever.

_____ B. Never have any chores.

_____ C. Receive complete understanding of all spiritual things.

_____ D. Have an incredible tan.

We're not quite finished with the Colossians verse, so let's read it again:

My purpose is that they may be encouraged in heart and united in love, so that they may have the full riches of complete understanding, in order that they may know the mystery of God, namely, Christ, in whom are hidden all the treasures of wisdom and knowledge. (Colossians 2:2-3)

If wisdom and knowledge of God is hidden, how can any of us know him? Earlier in this study, we talked about the Gnostics—which means "the intellectual ones." Paul directed this comment directly to them. Right now, we're reading the Bible in the English language. But if we were to read it in the Greek language, we'd see that the word Paul used for *hidden* is *apokruphos*. It means "hidden from the common gaze." Or in other words...secret. The Gnostics, remember, believed that you had to have incredible knowledge to receive salvation; you had to be extremely intellectual. They put all that knowledge down in books they called *apokruphos*, and they wouldn't allow ordinary people to have access to it.

In easy-to-understand terms, Paul is saying, "Yeah, you Gnostics hide your wisdom from common people. Well, Christians have knowledge, too! Only our knowledge is hidden inside Christ. And he's acceptable to everyone. Anyone can come to Christ and tap into his wisdom, knowledge, and plan of salvation."

In other words, the gospel is a secret that can be easily discovered in a personal relationship with Jesus himself. It's not a secret to remain hidden. Nor is it a secret available only to a select few. Every man and woman in the world can come to know Christ in all his fullness.

Rate yourself from 1 to 5 (one being not very good, and five being great) on how you're doing with the following:

✳   I have more knowledge of Christ today than I did a month ago.

    1   2   3   4   5

✳   I do specific things to promote unity in my youth group or Bible study.

    1   2   3   4   5

✳   I'm growing consistently in my understanding of Christ.

    1   2   3   4   5

✳   I have consciously worked to encouraged someone in the past week.

    1   2   3   4   5

✳   I'm good at making people around me feel welcome, loved, and cared about.

    1   2   3   4   5

✳   I'm striving to share the mystery of Christ with others.

    1   2   3   4   5

✳   I don't hide the fact that I'm a Christian.

    1   2   3   4   5

BITE #3

> I tell you this so that no one may deceive you by fine-sounding arguments. (Colossians 2:4)

Again, Paul is trying to help the Colossian Christians *guard* against the false teaching they were receiving. *Gnosticism* is religious heresy. In other words, it goes directly against biblical doctrine and attacks Christianity by teaching that important secret knowledge is *hidden* from most Christians. But remember what Paul said in Colossians 2:3?

...Christ, in whom are hidden all the treasures of wisdom and knowledge.

In Christ, we *can* discover all there is to know about Christianity. Young Christians who didn't know the Bible very well were easily swayed by this false doctrine and other false teachings. Imagine you're a "Bible Pharmacist." Write out a prescription for a confused Christian who is hearing false teaching.

The best way to understand Christianity is to know and understand the Bible. How's your Bible-reading? Are you consistent? Are you excited about studying God's Word? Jot down some things you'll gain from devouring the Bible.

If reading the Bible is tough for you, follow these tips:

* ***Get a Bible you understand.*** There are so many student Bibles available, you shouldn't have trouble finding one in a translation you can easily understand and one that's filled with Scripture helps, notes, and other spiritual growth boosters.

* ***Get a Bible you love.*** If you own a Bible you're proud of, chances are you'll carry it with you more and read it regularly. If you like a big Bible, shop for a big one. If you want something you can tuck in your pocket, purse, or backpack, you can find a small size. If you need lots of color and graphics to keep you moving through the pages, you can find a student Bible filled with eye-catching hooks. Make finding a Bible you love a high priority.

✱ ***Pledge to be consistent.*** If you're not used to reading the Bible every day, start with a short goal. Pledge to read the Bible for one minute each day. And ask someone to hold you accountable. You'll be surprised at the positive difference even one minute a day will make in your life.

✱ ***Mark it up.*** If a specific verse means a lot to you, underline it or draw an exclamation point by the side of it. If you don't understand a certain Scripture, put a question mark in the margin. Ask your youth leader—or another adult whom you trust spiritually—about it later. You can take advantage of the journal sections in this book to make notes about specific verses you don't understand.

For though I am absent from you in body, I am present with you in spirit and delight to see how orderly you are and how firm your faith in Christ is. (Colossians 2:5)

Paul praised the Colossian Christians who were *disciplined* and *solid* in their faith. Think about it: The more disciplined you are spiritually, the harder it will be for someone to come along and *confuse* you with false teaching or silly religious arguments.

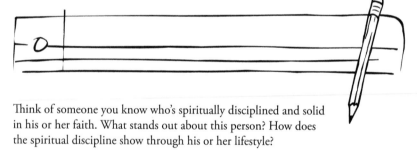

Think of someone you know who's spiritually disciplined and solid in his or her faith. What stands out about this person? How does the spiritual discipline show through his or her lifestyle?

In what ways do you need to be more disciplined spiritually?

What are examples of false teachings or silly religious arguments that tend to capture your attention, confuse you, or cause you to doubt your faith?

What needs to happen for you to solidify your faith and become all that God is calling you to be?

BITE #4

So then, just as you received Christ Jesus as Lord, continue to live in him, rooted and built up in him, strengthened in the faith as you were taught, and overflowing with thankfulness. (Colossians 2:6-7)

When you chose to follow Jesus, you were beginning a relationship with him—but it was merely a beginning point. Paul urged the Christians of Colosse to move forward in their relationships with Jesus. It's as if he's saying, "Now that you're started, keep going!"

Let's create a fiction scenario to illustrate this point.

Krissy was six years old when her dad brought home a kiddie pool, put it in the backyard, inflated it, and filled it with water. It was the perfect solution to those hot, sticky Texas summer days.

Krissy loved that pool! In fact, she splashed and played in it every single day. A few months later, she and her parents went camping. "Come on, Krissy!" her dad called. "I'll take you down to the lake to cool off."
Krissy excitedly followed her dad to the cool, greenish water nestled around the trees and tall grass. Mom helped Krissy with her life vest, and Dad held her hands as he walked her into the shallow water off the shore.

"I love it!" Krissy squealed. "I wanna swim."

"You don't know how to swim, honey," her mom said.

"But Daddy can teach me!"

So Krissy's dad gently began working with her and showing her how to kick her legs and move her arms. After an hour, Krissy was dog paddling by herself.

"Look at me, Mommy! I can swim!" Krissy screamed.

"You're doing great, honey," her mom said.

Flash forward a few years. Krissy is now 16 years old and hanging out at the pool with her friends in the summer.

"Hey, Ashley! Have you noticed that Krissy always stays in the shallow end of the pool?" Beth asked.

"Yeah. I've tried to get her to come further out and play Marco Polo with us, but she just stays in that one area. What gives?"

"I dunno. Let's go ask her."

"Krissy!" Beth screamed. "Come dive off the board with us."

"Nah, that's okay," Krissy said. "I just wanna float on my raft."

"Then bring your raft down here so you can hang out with us while we dive," Ashley said.

"Nah, I'll stay here."

Beth and Ashley got out of the pool and approached Krissy.

"What gives, girl?" Ashley said.

"Yeah. How come you always hang out in the shallow end?" Beth asked.

"I don't know. I guess I just like it here," Krissy said.

"Well...you can swim, can't you?" Beth asked.
"Of course I can! My dad taught me when I was six years old."

Okay, we'll interrupt the story right here. Can Krissy really swim?

_____ A. Yes.

_____ B. No.

_____ C. Yes and no.

_____ D. I'd hate to be drowning if she were the only person who was around
to save me.

> *Though Krissy **began** taking swimming lessons from her dad when she
> was six, she never **continued** those lessons. Yes, technically, she can paddle
> around in the water. But she'll never be able to **fully enjoy** the water—
> or venture into the **deep end** of the pool—until she takes more lessons. In
> other words, she needs to **continue** learning her water sport.*

It works the same way spiritually. You may have accepted Christ as your Savior, but
if that's as far as you go, you'll never experience a full, dynamic spiritual life. You'll be
hanging around in the shallow end of Christianity.

Jesus wants to move you away from casual Christianity! He wants to take you into
the deep end of the pool. Will you let him?

For you to go into the deep end of the pool spiritually, you'll need more lessons.
In other words, you'll need to continue growing spiritually. How can you grow
spiritually? (Check all that apply.)

_____ A. I need to read the Bible consistently.

_____ B. I need a raise in my allowance.

_____ C. I need to take swimming lessons.

_____ D. I need accountability.

_____ E. I need to belong to a Bible study or youth group.

_____ F. I need to go to the beach.

_____ G. I need to talk about what God is teaching me.

_____ H. I need to watch more TV.

_____ I. I need to pray consistently.

_____ J. I need to trust God with everything in my life.

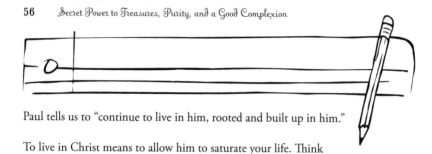

Paul tells us to "continue to live in him, rooted and built up in him."

To live in Christ means to allow him to saturate your life. Think about it: Is your life totally saturated with him?

What changes will you want God to help you instigate to make him truly the LORD of every area of your life?

The apostle Paul urges Christians to live in Christ and to be "rooted and built up in him." We automatically think of a tree whose roots have grown deep into the soil around it. The tree draws its nourishment through those roots. And the deeper the roots are, the stronger the tree is and the more likely it is to withstand strong winds.

Like a tree, Paul encourages us to grow our spiritual roots deep. The deeper our roots are, the stronger we are spiritually. And just as strong winds are unable to knock over giant trees, we can withstand the storms of life when our roots are deeply grounded in Christ.

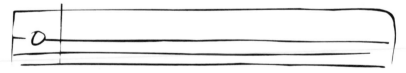

What are some of the most common "storms" that tend to knock you off balance?

Paul also encourages us to be "built up in him." Grab your Bible and flip over to Matthew 7:24-28. What analogy does Matthew use in this passage?

How does Matthew's passage compare with Paul's instructions?

Check out Colossians 2:6-7 one more time:

So then, just as you received Christ Jesus as Lord, continue to live in him, rooted and built up in him, strengthened in the faith as you were taught, and overflowing with thankfulness.

This verse ends with instructions to have what kind of attitude?

List the top 10 blessings for which you're thankful.

✳   ✳

✳   ✳

✳   ✳

✳   ✳

✳   ✳

How many people are on your gratitude list? Pause right now and grab some paper. Quickly scratch out a note of gratitude to each of the people on your list. Make it a point to either deliver these notes or mail them within the next two days.

BITE #5

See to it that no one takes you captive through hollow and deceptive philosophy, which depends on human tradition and the basic principles of this world rather than on Christ. (Colossians 2:8)

Is Paul saying that philosophy is bad? No. Paul, himself, was an incredible philosopher. But he is warning against any philosophy or religious teaching that goes against the Bible. People who don't make the time to study and understand God's Word are often lured into cults that *sound* religious but actually go against the Bible.

List some religions or philosophies that don't reflect the whole truth of the Bible and Jesus Christ as Lord.

For in Christ all the fullness of the Deity lives in bodily form. (Colossians 2:9)

Jesus isn't just a little piece of God Almighty. Yes, Jesus is God's Son, but Jesus is also fully God. All of God is found in Jesus Christ. When Jesus walked the earth, it was God walking the dusty roads in Jesus' body.

This truth is sometimes hard for our human minds to grasp: the deity of Christ and the trinity of God, Jesus, and the Holy Spirit. They're all one, yet they're distinct personalities. Perhaps this is something you'll ask God to help you understand better once you're in heaven. List the top five I Don't Get It questions you want to ask God when you spend eternity together.

1.

2.

3.

4.

5.

And you have been given fullness in Christ, who is the head over every power and authority. (Colossians 2:10)

Many of the Colossians were *curious* about other philosophies and religions. Paul wanted to remind them (and us) that when we know Jesus, we don't need to "try out" any *other religions* or get mixed up in cults. When we know Christ, we know God Almighty. When you accept Jesus as your Lord and Savior, you know GOD! You're on a first-name basis with the Creator of the universe. The King of Kings knows your name—and *calls* you by name!

Check out Isaiah 43:1 from *The Living Bible*:

But now the Lord who created you, O Israel, says, "Don't be afraid, for I have ransomed you; I have called you by name; you are mine."

How does it make you feel to know that God calls you by your very name? (Circle all that apply.)

ignored loved unique CARED FOR
ANGRY frightened valued
secure CONFUSED special LOST
found alone
the apple of God's eye excited focused
AMAZED

Paul also reminds us that Christ is *over* all other powers that exist. What are some other powers that exist today? (Check all that apply.)

_____   A. Political   _____   D. Satanic

_____   B. Athletic   _____   E. Money

_____   C. Celebrity   _____   F. Others

If we truly know Christ—who is more powerful than all other powers—why do we sometimes fear others who are powerful in our society?

BITE #6

In him you were also circumcised, in the putting off of the sinful nature, not with a circumcision done by the hands of men but with the circumcision done by Christ, having been buried with him in baptism and raised with him through your faith in the power of God, who raised him from the dead. (Colossians 2:11-12)

To understand why Jewish males were circumcised, we need to flip back to Genesis 17:9-14. When we read this portion of Scripture, we discover that circumcision was a symbol of the Jews' covenant with God.

The false teachers were telling the Gentile Christians in Colosse that they had to be circumcised in order to be Christians. (Gentile is simply a term for non-Jewish.) It wasn't the act of circumcision or cutting that saved someone. Circumcision was simply the *outer* sign of an *inner* commitment. True circumcision was much more than cutting a man's flesh; it was a *deep change* in one's *soul* that was reflected through his *lifestyle*.

Any priest could *physically* circumcise a man, but only God can bring about the change in a person's *heart*. Paul is saying the *change* is what matters—not the cutting of skin. Because Jesus came to earth and paid the penalty for our sins, his death canceled out the Old Testament covenant of animal sacrifice and male circumcision.

60 percent of male babies in America are circumcised today, but it's seen more as a *health* practice than a religious *custom*.

When you were dead in your sins and in the uncircumcision of your sinful nature, God made you alive with Christ. He forgave us all our sins, having canceled the written code, with its regulations, that was against us and that stood opposed to us; he took it away, nailing it to the cross. (Colossians 2:13-14)

According to the above Scripture, when did God choose to redeem you?

_____ A. After you cleaned up your act.

_____ B. When you joined the church choir.

_____ C. After you read the whole Bible.

_____ D. While you were still living in sin.

The *written code* that Paul mentions is the covenant mentioned in Genesis 17:9-14. The life and death and resurrection of Jesus Christ canceled out the old agreement of having to be circumcised to become saved. According to Colossians 2:13-14, of which sins has God forgiven you?

Let's take a peek at Colossians 2:13-14 from *The Living Bible*:

You were dead in sins, and your sinful desires were not yet cut away. Then he gave you a share in the very life of Christ, for he forgave all your sins, and blotted out the charges proved against you, the list of his commandments which you had not obeyed. He took this list of sins and destroyed it by nailing it to Christ's cross.

WOW! Take a few seconds to write a thank-you note to Christ for all he's done for you on the cross.

Think about it: God has not only forgiven your sins, he has chosen to completely forget about them! What's the first thing you want to say to Jesus when you enter heaven?

BITE #7

And having disarmed the powers and authorities, he made a public spectacle of them, triumphing over them by the cross. (Colossians 2:15)

When we ask Christ to forgive our sins, when we make him LORD, and when we live in obedience to his will, then we're in the process of becoming one with him. It's not just Christ who died; we die too. We "die" to our sinful natures. We "die" to our rights, our wills, our ways. Grab your Bible and check out Galatians 2:20. Describe what has happened to you—or is happening to you—according to this verse.

Because God has declared us not guilty, and because he totally rules our life, we no longer have to live under the power of sin. Yes, we'll still be tempted to sin, but with the Holy Spirit's power saturating us, we *can* choose to say no to temptation. We don't *have* to sin. When we're tempted, we can immediately pray for God's strength to say no.

What's your usual course of action when you face temptation?

Take a look at 1 John 2:1:

My little children, I write this to you so that you will not sin. But if anybody does sin, we have one who speaks to the Father in our defense—Jesus Christ, the Righteous One.

The apostle John reminds us that once we're living in the power of God's Holy Spirit we don't *have* to continue sinning. (See the *Secret Power Girl* book for more in-depth information on this lifestyle.) But because we're humans, we still might blow it. We still may sin from time to time. When we're Christians, and we do sin, what should happen next-according to 1 John 2:1?

_____ A. We should become a Christian all over again.

_____ B. We should throw in the towel. Christianity is too hard to actually live.

_____ C. We should live in solitude with no TV, computer, or other distractions.

_____ D. We should ask Jesus to forgive us.

Let's read Colossians 2:15 again:

And having disarmed the powers and authorities, he made a public spectacle of them, triumphing over them by the cross.

There's a high price tag on sin. How much does it cost? Death. But Christ paid that price for us when he died on the cross. When we "die" with him—when we give him our old lifestyle, our selfish desires, and our sinful nature—we no longer have to live in evil. We can truly enjoy our new life in Christ.

What are some of the biggest differences in your "old life" (before you were a Christian) and your "new life" (after you accepted Christ as your Savior)?

Do other people notice the difference in your lifestyle since you became a Christian?

Grab your Bible and flip to Ephesians 4:22-24. Describe the difference these verses paint between the "old life" and the "new life."

BITE #8

Therefore do not let anyone judge you by what you eat or drink, or with regard to a religious festival, a New Moon celebration, or a Sabbath day. These are a shadow of the things that were to come; the reality, however, is found in Christ. (Colossians 2:16-17)

What in the world is Paul talking about?

———— A. New Age stuff.

———— B. Birthday and Christmas celebrations.

———— C. Worship.

———— D. No one really knows.

———— E. Paul was in jail when he wrote this, so he was probably really tired and stressed and didn't know what he was saying.

Paul is talking about how we *worship*. Some Christians are more traditional in their worship; others are more contemporary. Today many Christians prefer a structured church service with hymns and liturgy; others enjoy worshipping through a fast-paced service filled with choruses, drama, and video. Instead of criticizing how someone worships *God*, we should simply concentrate on focusing our attention on Christ. After all, that's what worship is all about—focusing on Christ and giving him *praise*.

Describe your *preferred* style of worship. In other words, which methods best bring you into a mind-set of praise and attention to Christ?

Paul also told the Colossian Christians not to let people judge them because of what they were *eating*. In other words, don't base your *faith* (or hang out with people who base their faith) on *laws* that state some foods are spiritually "okay" and others aren't.

In the *Old Testament* days, specific foods were considered spiritually unclean, and God warned people not to eat certain foods. But when Jesus came, he *canceled* many of the Old Testament laws. The "unclean food law" was one he canceled through his death on the *cross*.

Did Jesus cancel ALL Old Testament law? *No.* The Ten Commandments were given to us in the Old Testament, and they're also mentioned in the New Testament. Christ "carried over" many Old Testament teachings into the *New Testament.*

The Old Testament is still *relevant* today! For us to become all God wants us to be spiritually, it's *essential* to study and understand the Old Testament as well as the New Testament. Jesus' life on earth didn't wipe out the Old Testament. In fact, Christ himself referred to the *Old Testament* and teachings from the prophets several times when he taught his followers.

Back to the food thing. Remember the Gnostics we mentioned earlier in this book? They were teaching false things and confusing many of the Colossian Christians. The Gnostics were big on combining religion with not eating certain foods. They considered all matter *evil.* Therefore food was definitely in the evil category—as well as most other things. But we know food is neither good nor evil. It's *amoral.* (That means neither moral nor immoral.)

It would be like you and your friends deciding that *chocolate* is evil, but *licorice* is okay. Imagine spreading this throughout your youth group and leading intense teaching seminars on this thought. It sounds crazy, doesn't it?

But pretend many in your youth group decided that what you said truly made sense, and they stopped eating chocolate and started eating more licorice. And imagine your youth group began to criticize other Christians for eating chocolate. "You're not really a Christian if you eat chocolate," you'd say.

What a commotion you'd stir! This is the kind of thing that was happening in the church at Colosse.

Though you probably don't hear many Christians criticizing others for what they eat, what *are* some things Christians criticize each other for?

What can you do to help Christians who criticize others?

BITE #9

Do not let anyone who delights in false humility and the worship of angels disqualify you for the prize. Such a person goes into great detail about what he has seen, and his unspiritual mind puffs him up with idle notions. (Colossians 2:18)

Remember the TV show "Touched by an Angel"? During the time it aired, angels were often talked about and angel paraphernalia became the rage. People were buying angel T-shirts, angel bookmarks, angel coffee mugs, angel everything! Many people put more thought and emphasis—and even faith—in the angels than in Christ himself. Yes, angels are real, but they are never to be worshipped. Only God is worthy of our worship.

It's time to get back to the Gnostics. Those false teachers were promoting that God was quite hard to reach. They taught that you had to go through several levels of angels to talk to God.

Check out one of the Ten Commandments found in Exodus 20:3-4:

You shall have no other gods before me. You shall not make for yourself an idol in the form of anything in heaven above or on the earth beneath or in the waters below.

Based on the above Scripture, what conclusion can you draw about worshipping angels?

Grab your Bible and flip to Revelation 22:8-9. What mistake did John make?

Whom was he instructed to worship?

Paul taught that when we know Christ, we have access to God the Father. Christ is our bridge. What are some common ways people try to reach God today? I'll get you started, and you fill in the rest of the list with as many as you can think of.

1. Spiritism

2.

3.

4.

5. Good works

He has lost connection with the head, from whom the whole body, supported and held together by its ligaments and sinews, grows as God causes it to grow. (Colossians 2:19)

Who is the "head" that Paul mentions in the above verse?

_____ A. The false teachers.

_____ B. Paul.

_____ C. Christ.

_____ D. Tom Cruise.

And who is "he" that Paul is saying has lost connection?

_____ A. The false teachers.

_____ B. Denzel Washington.

_____ C. The Green Bay Packers.

_____ D. Jo Mamma.

Throughout parts of the New Testament, the Church (made up of all Christians) is referred to as "the body." Christ is always referred to as "the head." Grab your Bible and check out 1 Corinthians 12:12-21. What do these verses tell you about the Body of Christ?

Now flip to Romans 12:4-5. What do these verses teach you about the Body of Christ?

Paul tells the Colossian Christians that those who are promoting false teaching are actually disconnected from the Body of Christ. They are no longer joined to the "head" or to Christ. Instead of receiving truth from Christ and passing it on to other believers, they created their own religious ideas and inflicted confusion and tension among the Christians. In what ways do you see people trying to create their own religious systems today?

Since you died with Christ to the basic principles of this world, why, as though you still belonged to it, do you submit to its rules: "Do not handle! Do not taste! Do not touch!"? These are all destined to perish with use, because they are based on human commands and teachings. (Colossians 2:20-22)

How does one become a Christian?

———— A. By following the basic principles of this world.

———— B. By submitting to specific religious rules.

———— C. By asking Christ to forgive one's sins and trusting in him.

———— D. By not eating certain foods.

Paul reminds the Colossians of their "death" to sin. When you gave your life to Christ, you "died" to your own rights and became alive unto him. In other words, your commitment says, "Jesus, I want your way and your will for my life—not my own."

Human laws won't last through eternity, but God's laws will. Be very careful, then, to whom you choose to listen. The ultimate voice is God, and you can read what God says in the Bible.

The biggest difference in false religious teaching and God's truth is that religions developed by humans draw our attention to us—our work—what we do and sacrifice. Christianity, however, focuses all of the attention on Christ and what he did on the cross.

Christianity can be described as...

_____ A. God reaching down to people.

_____ B. Something created by desperate people.

_____ C. People reaching up to God.

_____ D. People following religious regulations.

We can never reach God by following rules and regulations. We need to remember that it was God who chose to reach down to us. If God hadn't made that choice...

_____ A. We would have been forever lost.

_____ B. We would have eventually built a tower big enough to reach God.

_____ C. We would have found another god on another planet to die on another cross for us.

_____ D. We would have simply continued watching TV.

Such regulations indeed have an appearance of wisdom, with their self-imposed worship, their false humility, and their harsh treatment of the body, but they lack any value in restraining sensual indulgence. (Colossians 2:23)

Sixteen-year-old Jayme was admired by many students in her high school and youth group. She was just a really good girl. She never used bad language, never cheated on tests, respected her teachers, and reached out to new kids at school.

She attended church and youth group every week and often carried her Bible to school. In fact, it was Jayme's idea for the teens in her church to organize a fundraiser to buy the senior citizens a new van for their ministry days. She was fantastic!

Jayme was extremely disciplined too. She was a vegetarian, never drank soft drinks, and exercised every single day. She limited her TV intake to 30 minutes an evening and read four chapters from the Bible each week.

But Jayme had a secret.

Each night before she crawled into bed, she turned on her computer and logged into suggestive chat rooms. By using a fake name, she didn't feel guilty about the inappropriate comments she made or the flirtatious remarks she quickly typed.

Jayme was a completely different person when she was on the computer in the silence of her bedroom.

Now that you know Jayme's secret, what do you think about her?

———— A. She's a hypocrite.

———— B. She's confused.

———— C. She's pretending to be something during the day that's totally
opposite of who she really is at night.

———— D. She needs help.

Perhaps you marked all of the above. The *truth* is, many people are extremely disciplined and say impressive things, but that doesn't mean their *hearts* are right with God.

There are several religions that stress *discipline* and *good works*. But where will that get you? *No one* will enter heaven except through Jesus Christ—regardless of how disciplined or how good she *appears*.

Take a peek at John 14:6:

Jesus answered, "I am the way and the truth and the life. No one comes to the Father except through me."

When you hear Buddhists, New Agers, Muslims, Hindus, and others say, "There are many paths to heaven," how can you respond according to the above verse?

Though several other religions stress discipline and good works, those affect the outward actions and outward appearance of a person. God always stresses the condition of our...

———— A. Ribs.   ———— C. Heart.

———— B. Muscles.   ———— D. Brain.

God, and only God, can change a person's *heart.*

BITE #10
GRAB A FRIEND

Congratulations! You just completed the second chapter of Colossians. How does it feel to be a Secret Power Girl who is learning how to apply God's

Word to her life? Now grab a friend and discuss the following questions together.

✳ What treasures have I discovered in Christ this week?

✳ What specific things did I do to raise my spiritual temperature this week? (What am I doing to become an intensely "hot" Christian?)

✳ Paul deeply struggled for his loved ones. How have I demonstrated my love and burden for loved ones this week who don't have a personal relationship with Christ?

✳ What areas in my life do I claim to have "died to" when I came to Christ that I continue to struggle with?

✳ Like Jayme, is there an area in my life that's not consistent with Christianity?

MEMORIZE IT!

Try to memorize this verse with your friend and say it to each other the next time you get together:

So then, just as you received Christ Jesus as Lord, continue to live in him, rooted and built up in him, strengthened in the faith as you were taught, and overflowing with thankfulness. (Colossians 2:6-7)

MY JOURNAL

Okay, S.P.G. This is your space, so take advantage of it. You can do whatever you want with this space, but always try to include the following:

* List your prayer requests. (Later, as God answers them, go back and write in the date God answered your prayer.)

* Copy down any verse we studied in the previous chapter that you don't understand, and let this be a reminder to ask your parents, your Sunday School teacher, pastor, or youth leader about it.

* Jot down what stood out the most from this chapter.

Holiness Is Happenin'!

BITE #1

Since, then, you have been raised with Christ, set your hearts on things above, where Christ is seated at the right hand of God. Set your minds on things above, not on earthly things. (Colossians 3:1-2)

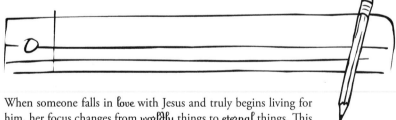

When someone falls in *love* with Jesus and truly begins living for him, her focus changes from *worldly* things to *eternal* things. This is part of *holy* living. What are some things you things you were focused on *before* you committed your life to Christ that just don't seem to matter anymore now that you're living for him?

Grab your Bible and read Matthew 6:19-21. According to this passage, where should we store our treasures?

What's the danger of storing treasures on earth?

What parallels can you draw from this passage and Colossians 3:1-2?

For you died, and your life is now hidden with Christ in God. (Colossians 3:3)

What does Paul mean when he says you "died"?

If your life is truly hidden with Christ, you'll...

_____ A. Never be found.

_____ B. Be seen as a reflection of him.

_____ C. Always eat Honeycomb cereal for breakfast.

_____ D. Get to heaven faster.

When you "die" to yourself, you allow Christ to saturate your life. And when he truly rules and reigns, you reside inside him. Others begin seeing Christ in your actions and reactions. They hear Christ in your words and feel him in your touch.

This type of commitment requires total surrender and learning to focus your thoughts and priorities on eternity instead of right now. When you live in total surrender to Christ, you begin living a lifestyle of holiness.

Are there times when you feel you don't fit in? Great! You're not supposed to. This earth is merely a temporary dwelling place for you. Your real home is heaven.

If your life actually reflected the truth that this life isn't what's eternal, what differences would it make in your attitude and choices?

BITE #2

When Christ, who is your life, appears, then you also will appear with him in glory. (Colossians 3:4)

How does this Scripture provide you with hope?

In this particular verse, Paul says that Christ is your...

_____ A. Father.   _____ C. Life.

_____ B. Eternity.   _____ D. Answer.

You may have a friend who's a terrific athlete. She's good at track, volleyball, basketball, and almost anything she tries. If she spends a lot of time with sports, you even may have said, "Sports is her life." What would you mean by that statement?

If Christ is truly your life...what should that mean?

Describe the difference between someone who's a casual Christian and someone who has surrendered everything to God and is living a life that's saturated in Christ.

Casual Christian:

Saturated in Christ:

Put to death, therefore, whatever belongs to your earthly nature: sexual immorality, impurity, lust, evil desires, and greed, which is idolatry. (Colossians 3:5)

How does the above verse reflect holy living?

Think about it: A dead person is unresponsive. So when you're tempted by the things Paul mentions above, what should your response be?

Since it's never easy to say no to temptation, what should we rely on for strength, help, and the empowerment to resist?

———— A. Our pastor.

———— B. A strong physical workout routine.

———— C. The Holy Spirit.

———— D. Vitamin supplements.

Check out 2 Corinthians 4:8-9 from *The Living Bible*:

> We are pressed on every side by troubles, but not crushed and broken. We are perplexed because we don't know why things happen as they do, but we don't give up and quit. We are hunted down, but God never abandons us. We get knocked down, but we get up again and keep going.

What encouragement can you draw from the above passage when it becomes tough to resist temptation?

BITE #3

Let's give Colossians 3:5 another read:

> Put to death, therefore, whatever belongs to your earthly nature: sexual immorality, impurity, lust, evil desires, and greed, which is idolatry.

Does it sound as if Paul is a killjoy? After all, God created us as sexual beings. So isn't it natural to have sexual needs and desires? From where do you receive most of your sexual messages?

———— A. Our pastor.   ———— E. Movies.

———— B. Friends.   ———— F. Magazines.

———— C. TV.   ———— G. Internet.

———— D. Music.   ———— H. Other: ————————

Though it's natural to have sexual needs and desires, God intended for those needs and desires to be expressed and met within the context of marriage. We're bombarded with sexual messages almost everywhere we turn. The world tells us to *fulfill* our sexual nature. Paul is telling us to *deny* it. What should you do when you're tempted?

_____ A. Face the temptation without yielding.

_____ B. Scream.

_____ C. Sing the theme song to "Gilligan's Island" very loudly.

_____ D. Run from the temptation.

Let's take a peek at 2 Timothy 2:22 from *The Living Bible:*

Run from anything that gives you the evil thoughts that young men [and women] often have, but stay close to anything that makes you want to do right. Have faith and love, and enjoy the companionship of those who love the Lord and have pure hearts.

We often think the way to handle temptation is by standing up to it. But according to Scripture, we're told to *run* from it. This is part of living a *holy* lifestyle. The apostle Paul wrote the above letter to *guide* and encourage his young friend Timothy, and we can use those words to guide us today.

With whom did Paul encourage Timothy to establish close relationships?

How can having these kinds of friends help us run from temptation?

Because of these, the wrath of God is coming. (Colossians 3:6)

The things Paul is talking about here are the *sins* mentioned in Colossians 3:5: "sexual immorality, impurity, lust, evil desires, and greed, which is idolatry."

According to Colossians 3:6, how does God feel about the above sins?

Paul uses the word *wrath* in Colossians 3:6. Identify other words he could have used in this same context:

Now, check out Joel 2:11:

The day of the Lord is great; it is dreadful. Who can endure it?

Though this verse is specifically referring to end times, it also gives us a glimpse into God's *judgment*. We know God is full of love and compassion, but we also know God is full of justice—and sin cannot be tolerated. We became part of God's family by asking for forgiveness us of our sins. And God was faithful to forgive us. The prophet Joel asks who can endure the Lord's judgment.

Guess what—*YOU* can!

But in Colossians 3:6, Paul reminds us that the sins mentioned in Colossians 3:5 will bring about the *wrath* of God. You'll never be free from temptation until you're in heaven. And as a growing Christian, you may stumble and give in to the temptation of one of the sins Paul lists. When that happens, then what?

———— A. I may as well forget Christianity.

———— B. I should seek forgiveness through Christ and continue my relationship with him.

———— C. I'll need to check myself into a psychiatric unit.

———— D. I'll move overseas.

Earlier in this book, we took a look at 1 John 2:1. Let's recap, okay?

My dear children, I write this to you so that you will not sin. But if anybody does sin, we have one who speaks to the Father in our defense—Jesus Christ, the Righteous One.

You don't have to give in to sexual immorality, impurity, lust, evil desires, or greed. You can claim the power of the *Holy Spirit* within you and say *NO* to these temptations. But if you do sin, John reminds us that we can go to Christ and seek *forgiveness*.

Christ will go to God on our behalf (Christ is our *bridge* to God), and tell the Father that we have repented, and that he has paid the penalty for our sin. At that point, God *erases the sin* and forgets!

This *truth* makes it possible for you to face the wrath or judgment of God. You can face it, because *you've been forgiven!* Therefore, when you stand in front of God, he'll stretch out his arms and welcome you into heaven.

But just because God will forgive your sins doesn't give you free license to sin!

Genuine repentance is NOT: I'll sleep with my boyfriend tonight, because I know God will forgive me when I ask for it later. (So you sleep with him and ask God to forgive you.) And I'll sleep with him again next Friday night, because I know God will forgive me again. That's not genuine repentance. That's game playing.

Genuine repentance IS: Oh, dear Father, I am so sorry I sinned. I realize my sin broke your heart. Will you forgive me? I don't ever plan on walking down that road again. In fact, I'll do specific things—set up certain boundaries and accountability— to make sure I don't go that direction again.

Create a fictional scenario that describes each of these attitudes.

BITE #4

You used to walk in these ways, in the life you once lived. But now you must rid yourselves of all such things as these: anger, rage, malice, slander, and filthy language from your lips. (Colossians 3:7-8)

Paul reminds the Colossians that though the above used to be part of their lifestyle, now that they're Christians, these things should have no place in their lives at all.

What things were part of *your* life before you became a Christian that you're still struggling to get rid of?

Of the things Paul lists, with which do you struggle the most?

_____ A. Anger (emotion).

_____ B. Rage (temper).

_____ C. Malice (evil).

_____ D. Slander (talking badly about someone).

_____ E. Filthy language (inappropriate words).

Since you're probably surrounded by filthy language (TV, movies, school), what can you do ensure you don't incorporate inappropriate language in your conversations?

Do not lie to each other, since you have taken off your old self with its practices and have put on the new self, which is being renewed in knowledge in the image of its Creator. (Colossians 3:9-10)

Paul talks about taking off your *old self* as you would take off dirty clothes. And he tells us to put on our new self—or new clothing. In New Testament days, new Christians were *baptized* by being totally immersed in water. This symbolized becoming totally immersed in Christ.

Imagine a person coming out of the water and tossing away her old clothes and putting on a clean, white robe. This is the obvious difference that Paul says our lives should show now that we belong to Christ.

But if we're still lying, cheating, and holding grudges, we're still wearing our old clothes; or we're still clinging to our old life.

Take a few minutes to write a eulogy (someone's brief life-summary after she's died—often found published in the newspaper), burying your old self and your old ways in Christ.

EXTRA! EXTRA!

THE DAILY NEWS
OBITUARIES

BITE #5

Here there is no Greek or Jew, circumcised or uncircumcised, barbarian, Scythian, slave or free, but Christ is all, and is in all. (Colossians 3:11)

One of the most exciting elements of Christianity is that it destroys the barriers between people. Hinduism places people in different castes, and someone in a lower caste can never be equal to someone in a higher caste. Aren't you glad that we can all be equals in Christ Jesus?

What are some of the barriers our society uses to distance people?

What barriers do you tend to place between yourself and others?

Therefore, as God's chosen people, holy and dearly loved, clothe yourselves with compassion, kindness, humility, gentleness, and patience. (Colossians 3:12)

This verse almost sounds as though God is asking you to participate in a *fashion show.* You're being asked to "clothe yourself" in qualities that reflect God's character.

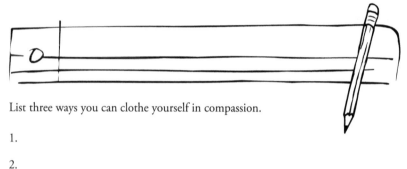

List three ways you can clothe yourself in compassion.

1.

2.

3.

What are three "random acts of kindness" you can perform this week?

1.

2.

3.

How can you demonstrate humility?

Have you shown gentleness in the past week? If so, describe how and when. If not, jot down how you *can* show gentleness.

How's your clothing of patience fitting? Is it a little too tight (patience wearing thin)? Or is it baggy—are you full of patience? Describe your P.Q. (Patience Quotient) in the space provided.

BITE #6

Bear with each other and forgive whatever grievances you may have against one another. Forgive as the Lord forgave you. (Colossians 3:13)

How did the Lord forgive you? (Check all that apply.)

_____ A. Completely.   _____ E. Arrogantly.

_____ B. Hesitatingly.   _____ F. Lovingly.

_____ C. Immediately.   _____ G. Wholeheartedly.

_____ D. With reservation.   _____ H. Begrudgingly.

What does it mean to "bear with each other"?

Describe a time when a friend or a family member granted you *forgiveness* when you really didn't deserve it.

How did it make you feel?

Describe a time when you have forgiven someone.

How did that person react to your forgiveness?

Let's look at a Scripture passage from another book Paul wrote. It's found in Ephesians 5:1.

Be imitators of God, therefore, as dearly loved children and live a life of love, just as Christ loved us and gave himself up for us as a fragrant offering and sacrifice to God.

What are the similarities in the above verse and Colossians 3:13?

When it comes to love and forgiveness, whom does Paul tell us to imitate?

In other words, this is a time when it's okay to be a copycat! So...how's your imitation coming?

When is it hardest for you to forgive?

When is it easiest for you to forgive?

If you struggle with forgiving those who have hurt you, stop and remember that God has forgiven you! Because of that, you shouldn't hesitate to forgive others. Is there someone you haven't yet forgiven whom God has placed on your heart? If so, write his or her name in the space provided and write out a prayer asking God to help you forgive this person.

BITE #7

And over all these virtues put on love, which binds them all together in perfect unity. (Colossians 3:14)

Think of as many virtues as you can, and list them in the space provided. I'll get you started.

gentleness

kindness

faithfulness

humility

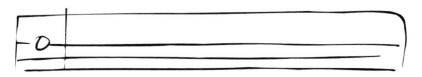

According to Colossians 3:14, what is the greatest virtue?

Grab your Bible and flip to 1 Corinthians 13:13. What three virtues does Paul say remain?

1.

2.

3.

What does he list as the greatest virtue?

Read Colossians 3:14 again. What is the result of love?

What kind of difference can genuine love make in a person's life? In a youth group? In a school?

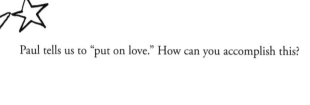

Paul tells us to "put on love." How can you accomplish this?

Let the peace of Christ rule in your hearts, since as members of one body you were called to peace. And be thankful. (Colossians 3:15)

What does it mean to let something *rule* your heart?

Who rules a baseball game?

_____ A. The players.

_____ B. The spectators.

_____ C. The umpire.

_____ D. The guys running the snack shack.

Just as an umpire rules a baseball game, Paul encourages us to let *peace* be the *umpire* of our *hearts*. Paul often uses athletic symbolism in his writing. Grab your Bible and read 1 Corinthians 9:24-27. What sport does Paul use in this analogy?

Now flip over to Hebrews 12:1. What athletic event comes to mind when reading this passage?

Now check out 2 Timothy 2:5 from *The Living Bible*:

Follow the Lord's rules for doing his work, just as an athlete either follows the rules or is disqualified and wins no prize.

What happens when an athlete doesn't follow the rules?

Now read Colossians 3:15 again:

Let the peace of Christ rule in your hearts, since as members of one body you were called to peace. And be thankful.

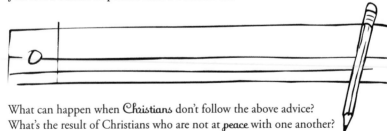

What can happen when *Christians* don't follow the above advice?
What's the result of Christians who are not at *peace* with one another?

It's interesting that Paul tells us to let peace rule in our *hearts*. Why do you think he mentions heart instead of *mind* or *actions* or *words* or something else?

Let's take a peek at Proverbs 4:23:

Above all else, guard your heart, for it is the wellspring of life.

How does this verse complement what Paul wrote in Colossians 3:15?

Paul ends Colossians 3:15 by telling the Colossians (and us) what?

_____ A. To be clean.

_____ B. To be thankful.

_____ C. To do our homework.

_____ D. To eat healthy.

Take a few moments to write a thank-you note to someone you appreciate but haven't told in a while.

BITE #8

Let the word of Christ dwell in you richly as you teach and admonish one another with all wisdom, and as you sing psalms, hymns, and spiritual songs with gratitude in your hearts to God. (Colossians 3:16)

From the very beginnings of the early Church, Christianity has a history of being a singing church. Christians would often spend hours singing praises to God. And remember, the early Church only had the Old Testament; the New Testament had not yet been written. Many of the stories about Christ and his teachings had to be memorized in order to be passed on. Sometimes these stories were set to music. It's no wonder, then, that music was an important part of the early Church. It was often used as a way to pass on information regarding Christian faith.

List three favorite praise songs you love to use in worship.

1.

2.

3.

Think of three favorite hymns you enjoy using in worship.

1.

2.

3.

List three favorite Scripture verses that help bring you into an attitude of worship. (You may want to use your Bible to find these and list them in the space provided.)

1.

2.

3.

And whatever you do, whether in word or deed, do it all in the name of the Lord Jesus, giving thanks to God the Father through him. (Colossians 3:17)

What does *whatever* include?

how I treat
a waitress
how I treat others
how I treat
tv
my job the jokes I tell
DRIVING chores MOVIES
sports THE MUSIC chat rooms
how I talk to my parents I LISTEN TO my free time
HOW I DRESS my hobbies my reactions
my friendships reliable habits relationships
walking my dog TEMPTATION
peer pressure
homework

Whatever includes not only all of the above...but even more! Whatever includes everything in your life and everything to come! Whatever is really...

_____ A. A foreign word to me.

_____ B. Something I hear a lot.

_____ C. All-inclusive of my entire life.

_____ D. A great name for what my school cafeteria serves.

Whatever requires *total submission.* It means everything in your life comes under God's control. Would you like to try a fun reminder of keeping whatever in your life under God's control? For the next two weeks, instead of greeting friends in your youth group or Bible study with, "Hi, how's it going?" try saying, "Whatever!" instead...with the understanding that whenever you hear "Whatever" it's a reminder that *whatever* you do, to do it in the name of Christ.

BITE #9

Wives, submit to your husbands, as is fitting in the Lord. (Colossians 3:18)

Thus far in Paul's letter to the Colossians, he's addressed the false teaching they were hearing, he's encouraged Christians to deepen their relationship with Christ—and he's explained how to do that—and now he moves into *relationships with other people.* And really, if Christianity doesn't affect our relationships with each other, there's a major problem. *Jesus* said the world would know we belong to him...

_____ A. By the kind of cars we drive.   _____ C. By our grades.

_____ B. By our love for one another.   _____ D. By what church we attend.

We can unpack Christianity and see it in action by how we live our lives! Paul begins with the home by telling women to submit to their husbands. Before you get annoyed and think, *I shouldn't have to submit to a man!*—let's take a peek behind the scenes in which this was written.

Under Jewish law, a woman was merely a possession of her husband—just like his animals, his house, or his land. She had no rights whatsoever. Also under Jewish law, a man could divorce his wife for any reason he created.

In Greek culture a woman with respect lived in seclusion. Her husband could go out as much as he wanted and could enter into a variety of relationships outside of his marriage, and no one would think less of him.

But the wife lived in a women's housing complex and didn't even join her husband for meals. She never went out on the streets alone—not even to shop for food at the market. Under both Jewish laws and Greek customs, all the duties fell on the wife's shoulders and all the privileges were granted to the husband.

Christianity changed this, in that Christian ethics promote a mutual responsibility in marriage. A genuine Christian man who allows God to truly saturate his life doesn't ask, "What can I get from her?" but rather, "What can I do for her?"

Yes, Paul tells women to submit to their husbands, but in the next verse he gives mutual responsibility to the man. Again, this went directly against the culture in which Paul lived. At that time, the husband was an unquestioned dictator in the home, and the wife was merely there to serve him, meet his needs, bear his children, and help them grow into responsible adults.

Let's move on to the next verse where Paul speaks directly to the men.

Husbands, love your wives and do not be harsh with them. (Colossians 3:19)

Paul is teaching that marriage becomes a partnership; that it not simply be something a man enters into for convenience, but rather a union in which a man and a woman find joy and completeness in each other.

Paul tells men to love their wives. What is God like again?

_____ A. Ruler.	_____ C. Magician.
_____ B. Lover.	_____ D. Judge.

In Bite #6, we talked about imitating Christ in everything we do (Ephesians 5:1). If husbands love their wives as God loves his children, they'll automatically be imitators of Christ. There's not a woman alive who wouldn't want to be loved by her husband the way Christ loves us!

And just how does Christ love us? (Circle all that apply.)

with hesitation **bitterly** ALL THE TIME
with a grudge ONLY WHEN sparingly
without fail ONLY WHEN HE HAS TO *unceasingly* **lavishly**
enough to die for us **joyfully** with open arms *once in a while*

Can you imagine a husband loving you this way? That's exactly how Paul is telling men to love their wives! That's how a Christian husband is supposed to love his wife. And when a man loves his wife this way—imitating how God loves us—a woman doesn't mind being submissive. She knows her husband has her very best interests at heart. She realizes her husband cares about her needs more than his own. She understands that he'd be willing to give his life for her. A woman would not be afraid or angry to be submissive to this kind of love.

Does this put a new spin on how you view submission in marriage?

Describe a couple you know who lives out this kind of marriage.

But Paul doesn't stop with the husband and wife. He continues with the entire family relationship.

Children, obey your parents in everything, for this pleases the Lord. (Colossians 3:20)

WHY should children obey their parents?

_____ A. Because parents are always right.

_____ B. Because children are stupid, and parents are smart.

_____ C. Because parents always know what's best for their children.

_____ D. Because this pleases God.

Grab your Bible and read Ephesians 6:1. What are the similarities in Colossians 3:20 and Ephesians 6:1?

In both letters, Paul never says children should obey their parents because they're always right. Parents aren't always right. They're human. They make mistakes. But God wants us to obey them because God has set up a specific position of authority. It works like this:

GOD THE FATHER

JESUS

PARENTS

CHILDREN

Just as Jesus continually obeyed his heavenly Father, we are to obey Jesus. He has placed parents in a position of authority over children, and he expects parents to teach children obedience, reverence, and honor.

Just as Jesus obeyed God, parents must obey Jesus, and children must obey their parents. Because parents are always right? No. But because that's the position of authority in which God has placed them.

In what area of obedience do you most struggle with your parents?

In what areas is it easy for you to obey your parents?

Paul continues to stress a *shared responsibility* throughout the entire family dynamic. He doesn't simply place everything on the wife's or husband's shoulders. Nor does he expect the children to be servants. He gives responsibility to *each* family member.

Fathers, do not embitter your children, or they will become discouraged. (Colossians 3:21)

Parents have a *tough* job! If they don't establish rules, chores, and discipline, their children can grow up to be *careless adults* without goals and maturity. But if parents expect too much, are always *nagging* their children, or rule with an iron fist, a child can become discouraged or even *rebellious*.

Paul encourages parents to find the *balance*. This is a process. It takes some adults longer than others. And there are always a *variety* of factors at play—environment, family history, insecurity, past abuse, and so on.

List four things your parents are doing right.

1.

2.

3.

4.

Write out a prayer for your parents in the space provided. Even though you may not always agree with them, you can thank God for them and pray for them.

BITE #10

Slaves, obey your earthly masters in everything; and do it, not only when their eye is on you and to win their favor, but with sincerity of heart and reverence for the Lord. (Colossians 3:22)

Paul is not condoning slavery, but he's stressing that our relationship with Christ should permeate all of our earthly relationships and transcend all barriers.

We could easily use this same Scripture for employee/employer relations. Perhaps you know someone who works hard when her employer is in the room but slacks off when he's gone. If so, she's not allowing her relationship with Christ to permeate her *work ethic.*

We could also use this same analogy for *household chores.* Do you work harder and accomplish a more thorough job when a parent is watching you? Do you still vacuum *underneath* the sofa and dust the tops of shelves even when they're *away*? This is simply good *ethics.* And Christians should have the *reputation* of a good work ethic.

Be honest. Evaluate your work ethic.

What kind of difference would it make in your part-time job, household chores, schoolwork, athletic training, or music practice if you did these things as if working for the Lord?

Remember, our *real* rewards aren't found in an allowance, a weekly paycheck, or earthly praise. Our real reward awaits us in heaven. Keep your eyes focused on the big picture—eternity.

Whatever you do, work at it with all your heart, as working for the Lord, not for men, since you know that you will receive an inheritance from the Lord as a reward. It is the Lord Christ you are serving. (Colossians 3:23-24)

Roman law stated that slaves couldn't own anything. Yet in this passage, Paul reminds us that all Christians will receive an inheritance from the Creator of the universe! Create a newspaper ad announcing your future inheritance:

EXTRA! EXTRA!   **THE DAILY NEWS**
ADVERTISEMENTS

Describe what it means to work at something with "all your heart."

Check out Clint's situation:

> *Central High School's football homecoming parade was a month away. Each class was responsible for constructing a float for the event, and the junior class had decided to create a giant boot with the slogan, "Warriors Kick to Victory!"*

> *As junior class president, Clint Calahan had called an after-school meeting to make plans to begin construction.*

> *"Jason's dad owns an empty field behind his shop we can use to build the float," he said. "We need everyone to help."*

> *"When would you like to begin?" Mrs. Johnson, the faculty sponsor asked.*

> *"This Saturday afternoon," Clint said.*

> *"I'll organize a group to bring sandwiches and cookies," Natalie volunteered.*

"Great. Let's all meet at Jason's at 1 p.m. this Saturday. Mike, you'll bring the plans and the drawing, right?"

"Yep," Mike said. "And Adam is in charge of assigning supplies to everyone."

"Okay. See you on Saturday!" Clint said as he closed the meeting.

Mrs. Johnson and several students followed Clint's example on Saturday as construction on the float began. Clint hammered, encouraged, passed out sandwiches, and painted.

When Mrs. Johnson's cell phone rang, and she left the area to talk privately, Clint stretched out on the grass and closed his eyes. "Whew! I'm drained," he said.

"C'mon, Clint! We've still got a lot to do," Mike said. "Get up and get over here, man."

"Like I said...I'm **tired**." And Clint fell asleep.

"Mrs. Johnson!" Natalie yelled as she saw the teacher approaching. "Look how much we've done!"

Clint bounced up and quickly grabbed a paintbrush.

"Wow! This is looking great!" Mrs. Johnson exclaimed.

"Yep. We've been working nonstop," Clint announced.

"I've got to run a quick errand," Mrs. Johnson explained. "But I'll be back in 15 minutes."

As soon as she was out of sight, Clint grabbed his cell phone and dialed his girlfriend. He propped his feet on the end of the float and leaned back in a wicker chair.

But when he heard Mrs. Johnson's car pull into the field, he quickly said, "Gotta go," and he slipped the phone into his back pocket. He then grabbed a hammer and some nails and started banging.

"Hi, Mrs. Johnson. Whatcha think?" he asked.

"I'm really impressed! In fact, I wouldn't be surprised if the junior class wins this year."

Many of the students approach you later and complain about Clint's work ethic. "You have to do something," they plead. "After all, you are the class vice-president!"

Based on Colossians 3:12-13 and Colossians 3:22-24, describe how you'll approach Clint and what you'll say.

Anyone who does wrong will be repaid for his wrong, and there is no favoritism. (Colossians 3:25)

Mark the following statements as true or false.

1. ＿＿ T ＿＿ F   God loves Asian people more than Indian people.

2. ＿＿ T ＿＿ F   Those who pay more tithe and give more in their church offerings get their prayers answered faster.

3. ＿＿ T ＿＿ F   God sees every action from every human being in the world.

4. ＿＿ T ＿＿ F   Though God sees actions, he can't know our thoughts...unless we choose to verbalize them.

5. ＿＿ T ＿＿ F   If someone gets by with something on earth, chances are good she'll also get by with it in heaven.

6. ＿＿ T ＿＿ F   God cares just as much about all of us doing our part on a homecoming parade float as about all of us doing our part on a church workday.

7. ＿＿ T ＿＿ F   God favors those who have gone to church all their lives over those who attend only a few times each year.

8. ＿＿ T ＿＿ F   There will come a time when everyone in the entire world is judged fairly by God.

When you feel a need to get even with someone, what advice can you draw from the above Scripture?

Grab your Bible and flip back to the Old Testament. Let's look at Deuteronomy 32:35. According to this Scripture, what will God do?

BITE #11

GRAB A FRIEND

Congratulations! You just completed the third chapter of Colossians. How does it feel to be a Secret Power Girl who is learning how to apply God's Word to her life? Now grab a friend and discuss the following questions together.

✱ How, specifically, have I handled temptation in the past week?

✱ Identify how you determined not to fit in with worldly things around you this past week.

✳ Describe the difference between genuine repentance and a casual attitude that says, "Ah, God will forgive me."

✳ Write about a situation in which you encouraged someone or forgave someone this week.

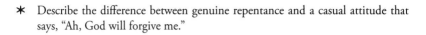

✳ Describe how you gave something *all your heart* in the past few days.

MEMORIZE IT!

Try to memorize this verse with your friend and say it to each other the next time you get together:

And whatever you do, whether in word or deed, do it all in the name of the Lord Jesus, giving thanks to God the Father through him. (Colossians 3:17)

MY JOURNAL

Okay, S.P.G. This is your space, so take advantage of it. You can do whatever you want with this space, but always try to include the following:

* List your prayer requests. (Later, as God answers them, go back and write in the date God answered your prayer.)

* Copy down any verse we studied in the previous chapter that you don't understand, and let this be a reminder to ask your parents, your Sunday School teacher, pastor, or youth leader about it.

* Jot down what stood out the most from this chapter.

Stuff To Grow On

BITE #1

Masters, provide your slaves with what is right and fair, because you know that you also have a Master in heaven. (Colossians 4:1)

Paul continues his theme of shared responsibility and a good work ethic among Christians. He reminds us that God is clearly the one in charge.

When is it most difficult for you to be fair?

Devote yourselves to prayer, being watchful and thankful. (Colossians 4:2)

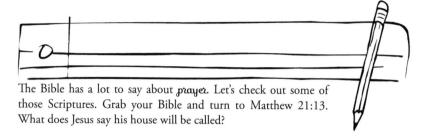

The Bible has a lot to say about *prayer*. Let's check out some of those Scriptures. Grab your Bible and turn to Matthew 21:13. What does Jesus say his house will be called?

Now take a peek at Proverbs 15:8. According to this verse, what pleases God?

And after reading Proverbs 15:29, you've discovered that God hears whose prayers?

What does Paul say the early Christians participated in together, according to Acts 1:14?

Romans 12:12 encourages believers to be patient in affliction and faithful in what?

According to 1 Corinthians 7:5, to what should we be devoted?

Check out 1 Peter 3:12. To what are the ears of God attentive?

Often when we pray, we tend to **ask** for things. But prayer should be a **two-way** conversation. This means...

_____ A. I should record my prayers and play them back later.

_____ B. I shouldn't be the only one talking. I need to also listen and allow God to speak to me.

_____ C. I should always listen to music when I pray.

_____ D. I should always pray with a friend.

Let's look at Colossians 4:2 again:

Devote yourselves to prayer, being watchful and thankful.

What two things does Paul tell us to do during our prayer time?

1.

2.

Watchful also means to be **alert**. Attentive. You don't want to be half asleep when the King of Kings speaks to you. So pray **expectantly**. Look for God's answers to your prayer. **Watch** and see how God works.

And instead of simply using prayer to **ask** for stuff, Paul encourages us to be **thankful**. Get into a good habit of thanking God for specific blessings every time you pray.

Take a moment right now to thank God for some blessings you've been given. Go ahead. Write your prayer of gratitude in the space provided.

Knowing that prayer is an essential part of a growing Christian's relationship with Christ, let's take a closer look at your personal prayer life.

_____ Yes _____ No   Have you experienced times when it seems as no one is really listening to your prayers?

_____ Yes _____ No   Have you ever received an answer to prayer?

_____ Yes _____ No   Have you ever prayed when you were desperate?

_____ Yes _____ No   Have you developed a consistent prayer life?

_____ Yes _____ No   Do you pray for others?

_____ Yes _____ No   Do you sometimes pray when you don't have a pressing need?

_____ Yes _____ No   Do you pray every day?

_____ Yes _____ No   Have you ever wondered about if your prayers are effective?

_____ Yes _____ No   Do you pray even when you don't feel like it?

Prayer is such an incredible privilege! Through prayer you have constant access to the Creator of the universe. And you can get through immediately! God doesn't have call waiting, and the line is never busy. When you call, God is there.

Stop right now and breathe a silent prayer—asking God to deepen your prayer life. Tell God your desire to talk more openly. Ask Christ to teach you the sound of his voice, so your prayers will be a two-way conversation.

BITE #2

And pray for us, too, that God may open a door for our message, so that we may proclaim the mystery of Christ, for which I am in chains. Pray that I may proclaim it clearly, as I should. (Colossians 4:3-4)

As you know, Paul was in *prison* when he wrote this letter to the Colossians. Isn't it interesting that as he's asking for prayer, he doesn't ask for release from jail, comfort, a speedy and positive trial, or better conditions. He only asks that the Colossians pray he'll proclaim the *gospel* as he should.

Wow! Paul was certainly focused on his purpose, wasn't he? All of us were created to bring glory to our Creator. The best way we can do that is by living a *lifestyle* that reflects Christ and by spreading his *message* in all circumstances.

Think about it: What kind of difference would it make in your life...if instead of asking God to *release* you from hard times, you instead asked God to *strengthen* you and grant you *endurance*? (Check all that apply.)

_____ A. Whoa! When I'm battling something, I want out as quickly as possible.

_____ B. Yeah, I can see how that would help me depend on God more.

_____ C. I'm not sure I *want* to learn and grow.

_____ D. Can I ask for endurance *and* release?

_____ E. That scares me.

_____ F. Wow! That gives me an entirely new perspective on how to face my trials.

_____ G. Yeah, I really *do* want to become all Christ desires for me to be, and if enduring something will help me become more like him, okay!

Check out what the apostle James says about facing tough times:

Consider it pure joy, my brothers, whenever you face trials of many kinds, because you know that the testing of your faith develops perseverance. (James 1:2-3)

Paraphrase (rewrite in your own words) the above verse in the space provided and insert your own name.

Let's take a look at James 1:2-4 from *The Living Bible*:

Dear brothers, is your life full of difficulties and temptations? Then be happy, for when the way is rough, your patience has a chance to grow. So let it grow, and don't try to squirm out of your problems. For when your patience is finally in full bloom, then you will be ready for anything, strong in character, full and complete.

What has a chance to grow during your problems?

What's the result of patience in full bloom?

Take a peek at Colossians 4:3-4 one more time:

And pray for us, too, that God may open a door for our message, so that we may proclaim the mystery of Christ, for which I am in chains. Pray that I may proclaim it clearly, as I should.

According to this Scripture, how was Paul "living out" James 1:2-4?

Why was Paul in chains?

How did Paul desire to proclaim the gospel?

———— A. On television.

———— B. Clearly.

———— C. With lots of publicity and fanfare.

———— D. Through the best sound system available.

Evaluate your personal approach to trials. When you're going through a tough time, how do you tend to respond?

According to Colossians 4:3-4, what should be your focus?

BITE #3

Be wise in the way you act toward outsiders; make the most of every opportunity. (Colossians 4:5)

No one enjoys being around a "know-it-all." While we should always be ready to share our faith with others, we have to be careful never to be critical of someone else's beliefs. We also need to remember, however, that not being critical isn't the same as acceptance. We can listen to opposing religious views, maintain a gentle spirit and lovingly share the difference Jesus Christ has made in our lives without accepting false teaching from others.

We should ask God for wisdom and discernment to know when to speak and when to be silent. Sometimes Christians think they should always be talking about their faith. But there ARE times when the Holy Spirit wants us to simply be quiet and live the life!

If we ask God to give us *specific* opportunities to share our faith, we'll get them! Paul is encouraging the Colossians to be *watchful* and to *recognize* when the opportunity arises to share their faith.

Think about your daily routine. What are some obvious *opportunities* you have for either *verbally* sharing your faith or living it "*out loud*" in front of someone by your actions?

Let your conversation be always full of grace, seasoned with salt, so that you may know how to answer everyone. (Colossians 4:6)

What do you think salty talk sounds like?

Salt gives *flavor* to our food and also helps *preserve* it. What are three things you absolutely would not want to eat without salt?

1.

2.

3.

Can you imagine eating chips or popcorn or fries with no salt? Salt makes things *taste* better. As a Christian, you should strive to make life *better* by the things you say and how you say them. Your *goal* should be to become a flavorful and godly Christian— one who *seasons* the lives of those around you with God's love and truth.

Grab your *Bible* and look at Galatians 5:22-23. This is a list of the fruit of the Spirit. How does living by the fruit of the Spirit enable us to be salty, *flavorful*, and influential to those around us?

Circle the words that are NOT reflective of salty conversation.

making fun
bitter *encourager* lies
CURSING Spirit BACK-STABBER treasure SARCASM
anger harsh going the extra mile *helper* *trustworthy*
self-centered
jerk FRIEND listener gossip
know-it-all joyful critical

Think about today. Take a moment to evaluate your conversation and actions. Were you mostly salty...or in need of salt?

BITE #4

Tychicus will tell you all the news about me. He is a dear brother, a faithful minister and fellow servant in the Lord. I am sending him to you for the express purpose that you may know about our circumstances and that he may encourage your hearts. (Colossians 4:7-8)

Paul ends his letter to the Colossians by mentioning several names. Again, we need to remember that Paul was imprisoned and in chains. The people he lists could be considered *heroes* of the Christian faith. It took lots of *courage* to visit someone in jail and to be known as a prisoner's *friend*. These people weren't worried about what others thought. They were clearly concerned about Paul and wanted to help him.

But who *was* Tychicus? He's also mentioned in *Acts* 20:4 and was from the Roman province of Asia. He was likely the *representative* from his church to take their offerings to the poor Christians of Jerusalem. He was also the one to deliver Paul's letter to the *Ephesians* (see Ephesians 6:1).

Paul says Tychicus will not only fill in the Colossians about what's happening, but he will also *encourage* their hearts. What a fantastic *reputation* to have! If someone were to place *labels* on you, what would those labels say? (Mark all that apply.)

Grab your Bible and turn to Acts 11:22-26. Who's known as the encourager in these verses?

Whom did he encourage?

How was he an encourager?

Whom does God want you to encourage this week?

He is coming with Onesimus, our faithful and dear brother, who is one of you. They will tell you everything that is happening here. (Colossians 4:9)

Who was Onesimus? He was a runaway slave. But Paul doesn't refer to him as a slave. Paul always strove to say the best about people. What does he call Onesimus?

Is there someone in your life about whom you always see the negative but should strive to see the positive? List some positive things about that person right now.

BITE #5

My fellow prisoner Aristarchus sends you his greetings, as does Mark, the cousin of Barnabas. (You have received instructions about him; if he comes to you, welcome him.) Colossians 4:10

Who was Aristarchus? He's also mentioned in Acts 20:4. *Aristarchus* was a Macedonian from Thessalonica. We don't have a lot of information about Artistarchus, but we *do* get some quick peeks at him. And through these fast glimpses, we can surmise that he was a good guy to have in your court when you were in *trouble*. He was known as a faithful and loyal friend who often risked his comfort for the good of the gospel.

Aristarchus was present when the people of Ephesus started a *riot* in the Temple of Diana. And whatever he did was so *noticeable* that he was captured by the mob. Flip to Acts 19:29.

According to this Scripture, who was also captured with Aristarchus?

Now check out Acts 27:1. This verse describes Paul as a...

_____ A. Celebrity.   _____ C. Tentmaker.

_____ B. Prisoner.   _____ D. Lion trainer.

Read Acts. 27:2. Who's with Paul as he's being shipped as a prisoner to Rome?

And now, according to Colossians 4:10, Aristarchus is in Rome with Paul as a fellow *prisoner*. Some Bible scholars believe that Aristarchus devoted himself to being Paul's *slave* in order to be with him always and encourage him.

Clearly, Aristarchus helped define the true meaning of *friendship*. It seems as though whenever Paul was in *trouble*, Aristarchus was with him as a faithful companion.

If your youth minister, pastor, or good friend was often in trouble for spreading the gospel, would you closely align yourself to him or her as Aristarchus did with Paul? Or would you be tempted to *keep your distance*?

BITE #6

Jesus, who is called Justus, also sends greetings. These are the only Jews among my fellow workers for the kingdom of God, and they have proved a comfort to me. (Colossians 4:11)

The Bible doesn't tell us anything else about Justus. We only know his name. But by reading Acts 28:17-29, we know the Jews in Rome didn't give Paul a hearty welcome. According to this passage in Acts, why did the Jews want to hear what Paul had to say?

How did Paul describe these people's hearts in Acts 28:27?

The Jews in Rome listened to Paul, but they *didn't* throw out the red carpet for him. But the men Paul mentions in the close of this letter to the Colossians were surely men who warmed his heart, encouraged him, stood by him, prayed with him, and supported him.

Epaphras, who is one of you and a servant of Christ Jesus, sends greetings. He is always wrestling in prayer for you, that you may stand firm in all the will of God, mature and fully assured. I vouch for him that he is working hard for you and for those at Laodicea and Hierapolis. (Colossians 4:12-13)

Who was *Epaphras*? He is thought to have been the *minister* of the Colossian church. (Flip back to Colossians 1:7.) He was also likely the *overseer* of churches in three different towns: Laodicaea, Hierapolis, and Colosse.

Paul says that Epaphras has been *wrestling* in prayer. In Colossians 1:29, Paul mentioned that he, himself, had been struggling in *prayer*.

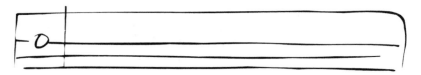

Why does it sometimes seem as though prayer is a struggle or a wrestling match?

Grab your Bible and flip to Genesis 32:22-32. Who was wrestling with God in prayer throughout these verses?

At the end of this wrestling match, to what did God change this man's name?

BITE #7

> Our dear friend Luke, the doctor, and Demas send greetings. Give my greetings to the brothers at Laodicea, and to Nympha and the church in her house. (Colossians 4:14-15)

Luke was a *physician* who wrote the Gospel of Luke. As you read his Gospel and compare it with the other three Gospel accounts, you'll notice that Luke was extremely *detail-oriented* and took great care in preserving many pieces of information. As a man of *science*, he began his book by outlining his extensive *research* and facts. He was a dependable friend to Paul. One has to wonder if he possibly gave up a moneymaking career in medicine to help Paul.

Read 2 Corinthians 12:7. What negative thing is Paul battling?

Did Dr. Luke forsake his medical career to travel with Paul and possibly tend to his "thorn in the flesh"? We don't know for sure. But we do know that he was a faithful supporter of Paul. Check out 2 Timothy 4:11. Who is with Paul until the end?

After this letter has been read to you, see that it is also read in the church of the Laodiceans and that you in turn read the letter from Laodicea. (Colossians 4:16)

The letter to Laodicea was lost, and that's why it's not included in the Bible. But this verse reminds us of the importance of verbal instruction in Paul's day. Because they didn't have fancy printing presses or computers, word of mouth was considered an important means of spreading news.

Perhaps you're familiar with stories of P.O.W.s or imprisoned missionaries who didn't have access to a Bible and had to rely on Scripture memorization. Strive to make Scripture memory an important part of your Christian life. After you have memorized a Scripture from the Bible, the Holy Spirit will be faithful to bring it to your mind when you need it.

In the space provided, write out a verse of Scripture that you have memorized.

BITE #8

Tell Arcippus: "See to it that you complete the work you have received in the Lord." (Colossians 4:17)

It's often easy to *start* something and leave before it's *completed*. Which of the following areas is it tempting for you to walk away without completion?

_____ A. Homework.		_____ f. Practicing the piano.
_____ B. Household chores.		_____ g. A movie.
_____ C. Conflict.		_____ h. Exercise.
_____ D. A television show.		_____ i. Taking medicine.
_____ E. Bible reading.		

Have you ever stopped to think about what would happen if God got bored and decided not to *complete* what he started? What if Jesus had climbed off the cross and not completed the payment for our sins? God is a God of completion, and God wants us all to give our full attention to completing the tasks set before us.

Check out Philippians 1:4-6:

In all my prayers for all of you, I always pray with joy because of your partnership in the gospel from the first day until now, being confident of this, that he who began a good work in you will carry it on to completion until the day of Christ Jesus.

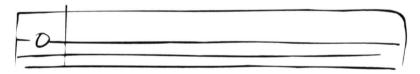

According to the above Scripture, who began a good work in you?

Who is committed to carrying it on until completion?

Since Christ is committed to completing his work in you, will you also commit to completing the tasks and opportunities he brings your way? If so, create a *completion pledge* in the space below that reflects your desire to be a *finisher.*

I, Paul, write this greeting in my own hand. Remember my chains. Grace be with you. (Colossians 4:18)

Paul knew he was *ineffective* without prayer. By mentioning his chains, he's reminding the Colossians to continue praying for him during his imprisonment. Paul was acutely aware of his dependence on Christ and how much he *needed* the prayers of fellow Christians. Who is depending on *your* prayers?

 For whom should you be praying daily?

Will you **commit** to praying for missionaries and others who are faithfully spreading the gospel? You may never see these people, but you can actually aid in the *effectiveness* of their ministry by praying consistently for them!

BITE #9

GRAB A FRIEND

Congratulations! You just completed the fourth chapter of Colossians. How does it feel to be a Secret Power Girl who is learning how to apply God's Word to her life? Now grab a friend and discuss the following questions together:

* What are some earthly treasures I have placed more emphasis on this week than I should have?

* In what specific situations did I ask God for endurance this week instead of deliverance in my trials?

* What opportunities did I use this week to share my faith? Any missed opportunities?

* How did I specifically flavor my speech and actions with saltiness and a positive influence this past week? In what areas did I need some salt on my words?

* Paul closed his letter by naming several faithful friends. To whom and how have you been a faithful friend this week?

MEMORIZE IT!

Try to memorize this verse with your friend and say it to each other the next time you get together:

Devote yourselves to prayer, being watchful and thankful. (Colossians 4:2)

MY JOURNAL

Okay, S.P.G. This is your space, so take advantage of it. You can do whatever you want with this space, but always try to include the following:

* List your prayer requests. (Later, as God answers them, go back and write in the date God answered your prayer.)

* Copy down any verse we studied in the previous chapter that you don't understand, and let this be a reminder to ask your parents, your Sunday School teacher, pastor, or youth leader about it.

* Jot down what stood out the most from this chapter.

P.S.: The **title** of this book promises you'll learn about God's treasures, purity, and a good complexion. Briefly describe what you've discovered about finding treasures in Christ.

Now in a short paragraph, describe what you've learned about being pure in Christ.

Okay. Now it's time to chat about a good complexion. We've talked a lot about being an encourager, being kind, going the extra mile, and being a faithful friend in this book. Guess what? If you'll actually live out those qualities, you'll develop a complexion that will automatically draw others to you!

See, there's more than one kind of complexion. We tend to think of a facial complexion, but we also have a character complexion. If you've truly completed this study and are taking to heart what you've learned, you're in the process right now of developing a good complexion—one that's a clear reflection of Christ himself. Major congrats!

Do you hate looking at yourself in the mirror?

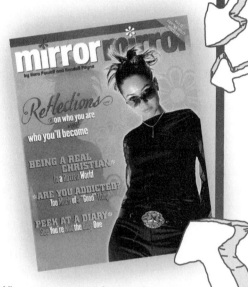

When you see your image, do you see everything that is wrong with you? Hair that doesn't look right or a body that you don't want? *Mirror, Mirror* is packed with raw honesty and truth, not easy answers or packaged solutions. It will help you think deeper about beauty, self-image, acceptance, health, sex, God's love, and more.

RETAIL $12.99
ISBN 0310248868

invert

How do you see yourself? How does God see you? Super models, positive thinking, self-help books, diets, cosmetics, dating guides—they are all supposed to make you more self-assured. But they often wind up leading to confusion, disappointment, and insecurity.

secret power
for girls
Identity, Security, and Self-Respect in Troubling Times
susie shellenberger

Secret Power for Girls addresses important questions you have about yourself and about your image and gives you answers, help, and strength.

invert